Lesotho: A Development Challenge

This report is based on the findings of an economic mission to Lesotho in June/July 1973, composed of Messrs. Willem Maane (mission chief) and Robert van der Lugt (general economist), and a follow-up mission in March 1974 by Mr. Willem Maane, who is responsible for the scope and overall conclusions of the report.

The World Bank
Washington, D.C., U.S.A.

Library of Congress Cataloging in Publication Data:

International Bank for Reconstruction and Development.

Lesotho: a development challenge.

"This report is based on the findings of an economic mission to Lesotho in June/July 1973, composed of Messrs. Willem Manne (mission chief) and Robert van der Lugt (general economist), and a follow-up mission in March 1974 by Mr. Willem Maane, who is responsible for the scope and overall conclusions of the report."

1. Lesotho—Economic conditions. I. Maane, Willem, 1927- II. Title.

HC517.L4I58 330.9'68'603 75-30508

ISBN 0-916058-06-9

The World Bank issues country economic reports in two series. This report is a working document and is, as such, part of an informal series wholly based on materials prepared for restricted use within the Bank. The text is not meant to be definitive, but is offered so as to make some results of internal research widely available to scholars and practitioners throughout the world.

The Bank maintains a continuing program to expand the scope and strengthen the quality of all social and economic statistics used in its operations and research activities. Some of these data are published routinely in the *World Bank Atlas,* the *World Bank Annual Report,* and *Trends in Developing Countries.* Other statistical series maintained by the Bank and used almost exclusively by Bank staff are published only infrequently.

The *World Bank Catalog* lists all of the Bank's free and sale publications; it is available to any individual or institution with a serious interest in economic and social development. To obtain more information about Bank publications and to request a copy of the *Catalog,* contact the Publications Unit, World Bank, 1818 H Street, N.W., Washington, D.C. 20433 U.S.A., or the World Bank, 66 avenue d'léna, 75116 Paris, France.

Other titles in this working document series of country reports may be ordered from either the Washington or Paris offices; currently available are:

Employment in Trinidad and Tobago
(March 1973)

Current Economic Position and Prospects of Ecuador
(October 1973)

Current Economic Position and Prospects of Peru
(December 1973)

Chad: Development Potential and Constraints
(1974 — ISBN 0-916058-00-X)

Le Développement du Tchad: Possibilités et Limites
(1974 — ISBN 0-916058-03-4)

Senegal: Tradition, Diversification, and Economic Development
(1974 — ISBN 0-916058-01-8)

Sénégal: Tradition, Diversification et Développement Economique
(1974 — ISBN 0-916058-05-0)

Turkey: Prospects and Problems of an Expanding Economy
(1975 — ISBN 0-916058-04-2)

The second series of country reports is published for the World Bank by The Johns Hopkins University Press. Individual titles currently available may be obtained in clothbound and paperback editions from bookstores, The Johns Hopkins University Press (Baltimore, Maryland 21218, U.S.A.), or its agents:

Economic Growth of Colombia
(1972 — ISBN 0-8018-1389-1 / 0-8018-1397-2)

Nigeria: Options for Long-Term Development
(1974 — ISBN 0-8018-1602-5 / 0-8018-1603-3)

Yugoslavia: Development with Decentralization
(1975 — ISBN 0-8018-1702-1 / 0-8018-1715-3)

Kenya: Into the Second Decade
(1975 — ISBN 0-8018-1754-4 / 0-8018-1755-2)

PERTINENT DATA

The country :	Lesotho
The people :	Mosotho (singular)
	Basotho (plural)
The language:	Sesotho

Currency Equivalents as of June 1974

US$1 = Rand 0.67
Rand 1 = US$1.49

Weights and Measures

1 mile	=	1.609 kilometers
1 kilometer	=	0.621 miles
1 acre	=	0.405 hectares
1 hectare	=	2.47 acres
1 bag = 200 lb.	=	90.74 kilograms

Fiscal year

April 1-March 31

GLOSSARY

ADF	Agricultural Development Fund
BAFED	Basutoland Factory Estates Development Company
BEDCO	Basotho Enterprises Development Corporation
CIDA	Canadian International Development Agency
DANIDA	Danish International Development Agency
ESCOM	Electricity Supply Commission of South Africa
FAO	Food and Agriculture Organization
ILO	International Labour Organisation
IPPF	International Planned Parenthood Federation
ITU	International Telecommunications Union
LAC	Lesotho Airways Corporation
LCH	Lesotho Cooperative Handicrafts Society
LEC	Lesotho Electricity Corporation
LECUSA	Lesotho Credit Union Scheme for Agriculture
LIBA	Lesotho Institute for Business and Administration
LNDC	Lesotho National Development Corporation
LTI	Lerotholi Technical Institute
NTTC	National Teacher Training College
ODA	Overseas Development Assistance
OXFAM	Oxford Relief Fund
POSB	Post Office Savings Bank
SIDA	Swedish International Development Agency
UBLS	University of Botswana, Lesotho, and Swaziland
Unesco	United Nations Educational, Scientific, and Cultural Organization
UNDP	United Nations Development Programme
USAID	U.S. Agency for International Development
VIDO	Village Industries Development Organization

TABLE OF CONTENTS

LIST OF TEXT TABLES

COUNTRY DATA - LESOTHO

AREA
30,340 sq. km.

POPULATION
1.2 million (mid-1973)1/
Rate of growth: 2.2% a year

DENSITY
38 per sq. km.
280 per sq. km. of arable land

POPULATION CHARACTERISTICS (1968/69)	
Crude birth rate (per 1,000)	37
Crude death rate (per 1,000)	15
Infant mortality (per 1,000 live births)	106

INCOME DISTRIBUTION (1972)	
% of national income, lowest quintile	15
highest quintile	33

DISTRIBUTION OF LAND HOLDERSHIP (1970)2/	
% held by the top 10% of holders	22
% held by the bottom 10% of holders	3

DISTRIBUTION OF CATTLE OWNERSHIP (1970)	
% owned by the top 10% of owners	16
% owned by the bottom 10% of owners	7

ACCESS TO PIPED WATER	
% of population - urban	..
- rural	..

ACCESS TO ELECTRICITY	
% of population - urban	..
- rural	..

HEALTH (1972)	
Population per physician	22,600
Population per hospital bed	600

NUTRITION	
Calorie intake as % of requirements	..
Per capita protein intake	..

EDUCATION (1973)	
Adult literacy rate %	40
Primary school enrollment %	64
Secondary school enrollment %	6

GNP PER CAPITA IN 1971: about US$100

GROSS NATIONAL PRODUCT IN 1970/71 / ANNUAL RATE OF GROWTH (%, constant prices)

	US$ Mln.	%	1960-65	1965-70
GNP at market prices	86.8	100.0	..	0
Gross domestic investment	7.0	8.1	..	0
Gross national savings	-4.9	-5.6	.	.
Current account balance	..		.	.
Exports of goods	16.8	19.4	..	..
Imports of goods	49.7	57.3	..	-3

OUTPUT, LABOR FORCE AND PRODUCTIVITY IN 1970/71

	Value added US$	Value added %	Labor force3/ Thousand	Labor force3/ %	V.A. per worker US$	V.A. per worker %
Rural sector	35.8	60.2	227	91	160	67
Industry	3.2	5.4	3	1	1000	417
Services	20.5	34.4	20	8	1000	417
Total/Average	59.5	100.0	250	100	240	100

GOVERNMENT FINANCE

	Central Government: Rand Mln 1972/73	% of GDP 1972/73	% of GDP 1966/67-1971/72
Current receipts	12.0	24.0	16.3
Current expenditure	13.8	27.6	25.2
Current surplus	-1.8	-3.6	-8.9
Capital expenditures	3.1	6.2	6.1
External assistance (net)	2.7	5.7	14.1

1/ Including an estimated 200,000 Basotho migrant workers in South Africa.

2/ Refers to arable land held under traditional tenure arrangements.

3/ Excluding migrant workers.

.. not available
. not applicable
- zero or negligible

COUNTRY DATA - LESOTHO

MONEY, CREDIT AND PRICES	1965	1969	1970	1971	1972	June 1973
		(Million Rand outstanding end period)				
Money and Quasi Money	..	..	..	..	..	..
Bank Credit to Public Sector	..	0.1	0.1	0.1	0.2	0.4
Bank Credit to Private Sector	..	1.9	2.6	4.3	4.8	4.9
		(Percentages or Index Numbers)				
						1973
General Price Index (1963 = 100)[1/]	105.9	116.1	119.7	125.7	134.6	150.1
Annual Percentage Changes in:						
General Price Index	3.3	2.2	3.1	5.0	7.1	11.5
Bank Credit to Public Sector	..	..	0	0	100	..
Bank Credit to Private Sector	..	..	37	65	12	..

BALANCE OF PAYMENTS

	1970	1971	1972
	(million Rand)		
Recorded Exports of Goods	4.2	-3.0	-6.1
Recorded Imports of Goods	22.9	28.0	43.0
Recorded Trade Deficit	-18.7	-25.0	-36.9
Interest Payments (net)	..	..	..
Workers' Remittances	15.0	16.0	17.0
Other Factor Payments (net)	..	..	..
Net Transfers	..	..	..
Balance on Current Account	..	..	..
Direct Foreign Investment	..	..	..
Net MLT Borrowing	0.0	0.0	0.0
Capital Grants	2.5	3.6	2.1
Other Items n.i.e.	..	..	..
Increase in Reserves (+)	.	.	.

MERCHANDISE EXPORTS (AVERAGE 1970-72)

	R. Mlns.	%
Live Animals	0.8	18.2
Foodstuffs	0.7	15.9
Wool and Mohair	2.0	45.4
Diamonds	0.4	9.1
All other Commodities	0.5	11.4
Total	4.4	100.0

EXTERNAL DEBT, DECEMBER 31, 1972

	US$ Mln.
Public Debt, incl. Guaranteed	8.3
Non-guaranteed Private Debt	..
Total Outstanding & Disbursed	8.3

DEBT SERVICE RATIO FOR 1972[2/]

	%
Public Debt, incl. Guaranteed	2.4
Non-guaranteed Private Debt	..
Total Outstanding & Disbursed	2.4

RATE OF EXCHANGE

Through - 1971
US$1.00 = R0.71
R1.00 = US$1.40

Since June 1973
US$1.00 = R0.67
R1.00 = US$1.49

Dec. 1971 - May 1973
(Average for period)
US$1.00 = R0.76
R1.00 = US$1.31

IBRD/IDA LENDING, (DEC. 1973) (Million US$)

	IBRD	IDA
Outstanding & Disbursed	-	5.0
Undisbursed	-	5.6
Outstanding incl. Undisbursed	-	10.6

1/ Average of South African wholesale and consumer price indices.

2/ Ratio of debt service to government current revenue

.. not available
. not applicable
- zero or negligible

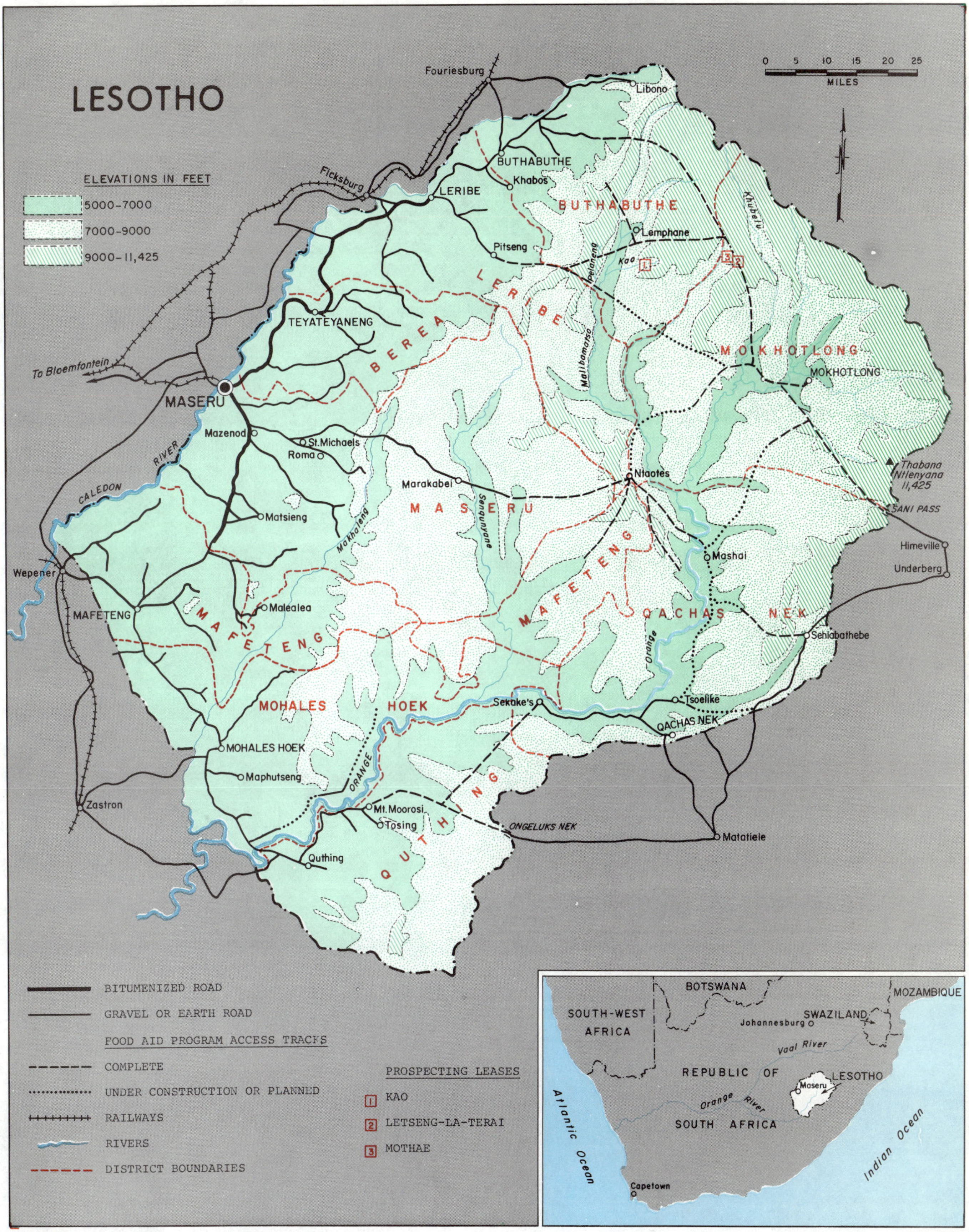

JUNE 1971 IBRD-3506

Lesotho: A Development Challenge

SUMMARY AND CONCLUSIONS

A. The Economic Scene

The Kingdom of Lesotho is a small, overpopulated country, surrounded by South Africa on all sides. It is very poor and desperately short of natural resources. Traditional rural activities provide an important source of income for about 85 percent of the people. Not more than 13 percent of the country is suited to crop cultivation; the rest is mountainous and suitable only for grazing. Rapid population growth, deteriorating soil, and declining agricultural yields have over the years led to a situation in which the country was no longer able to provide enough food for its people. Many able-bodied men left the land, but the only employment opportunities were in neighboring South Africa. At present an estimated 60 percent of the male labor force is away as migrant workers in South Africa.

Wages in South Africa, even those of unskilled workers, are much higher than prospects of agricultural earnings in Lesotho. The South African labor market, therefore, has exerted a strong pull which, conversely, has contributed to the decline in agricultural productivity in Lesotho. The strong economic reasons for working in South Africa are reinforced by sociological reasons. Working in South Africa, in particular working in the mines, has penetrated into Lesotho culture. Having been in the mines is now one of the ways in which a young Mosotho proves his manhood. However, the social cost of migrant labor -- i.e., disrupted family life -- is undoubtedly high.

Lesotho has acute soil erosion problems. About half of the cultivated areas and mountain pastures are affected in various degrees. The government has long since tried to stem erosion by constructing conservation works, but these attempts were not tied in with any agricultural production schemes. Bad farming practices continued, which caused serious further erosion. Only recently have rural development projects been evolved which hold out hope that what remains of Lesotho's soil can be saved.

Apart from its soil, Lesotho has few other known natural resources. The only abundant natural asset, which is not being tapped yet, is water in the mountains. A feasibility study has been prepared for a project to export large quantities of water to South Africa. The potential for irrigation has not been investigated comprehensively, but what studies there are suggest that it is limited. Mining has so far been confined to some small-scale diamond digging. A medium-size mine is about to be established. Another natural asset which is still largely unexploited is Lesotho's beautiful mountain scenery. Consultants have prepared a report on the country's tourism potential.

Together with South Africa, Botswana, and Swaziland, Lesotho belongs to the rand monetary area and the Southern African Customs Union. Movement of goods and funds within the area is virtually free. Lesotho has no central bank of its own, and the South African rand circulates as legal tender. This situation has both advantages and disadvantages for Lesotho.

The disadvantages of the arrangements are mainly that they severly limit the set of policy instruments normally available to independent countries. Although in theory the arrangements provide for consultation among the participating countries, in practice it has been South Africa who has determined the policies related to foreign exchange, exchange rates, monetary matters, and levels of customs, excise, and sales taxes. These policies are generally determined in the light of South African economic conditions and are not necessarily in the best interest of the three smaller countries.

A potential advantage of the arrangements is the duty-free access that Lesotho's industries have to a large market with great purchasing power. Lesotho, however, has not yet been able to benefit substantially from this situation. There is a natural tendency towards polarization of industrial development in areas which are already industrially advanced, all of which are in South Africa. What is more, existing administrative and cartel arrangements in South Africa have, in spite of the principle of a free flow of goods, acted as a deterrent to the establishment of large-scale industries in Lesotho. Lesotho, together with Botswana and Swaziland, need to keep the customs union arrangements and South African trading practices under constant scrutiny in order to identify defects and to take steps to protect their interests.

Lesotho receives a proportion of the total customs and excise revenue of the whole customs area, which accounts for a substantial part of its recurrent revenue. Since the renegotiation of the customs agreement in 1969, Lesotho has received a significant increase in its share, not only because of the new agreement itself, but also because of better recording of imports, the level of which determines Lesotho's share in the common customs and excise pool.

Lesotho's economic ties to South Africa go far beyond the monetary and customs arrangements. South Africa is Lesotho's main trading partner. South African companies and individuals dominate not only foreign trade but also internal wholesale and retail business. Also, South Africa has traditionally provided employment to a large portion of Lesotho's labor force. Lesotho derives significant benefits from this in the form of remittances; but, on the other hand, the fact that there is almost no permanent core of male labor hampers agricultural development.

B. Economic Trends

Economic indicators for Lesotho are scarce and unreliable. The government's own budget statistics are the only reliable information available. Production statistics are virtually nonexistent. Whatever indicators there are, however, all point to poverty and stagnation over a long period of time, reflecting the country's poor natural resources and lack of development in the past. The rural sector contributes about 60 percent of GDP. The other productive sectors are all very small. Manufacturing, mining, construction, and public util es together contribute probably not more than 5 percent of GDP. Agricu ural censuses held in 1950, 1960, and 1970 suggest a steady declin in production over the last two decades. Manufacturing output is estimated   ave tripled since 1967, but its contribution to GDP is still insigni icant. Available statistics suggest that, in real terms, total GDP per capita has fallen slightly over the last decade or so; but this decrease has been compensated by an increase in remittances from migrant workers. Per capita GNP, therefore, may have remained more or less stable at US$100.

The level of gross fixed investment is estimated to have remained at some R5 million a year (about 10 percent of GDP) since independence. About half of this would have been investment by the government and public enterprises, and the rest represents investment by private enterprises and missions as well as investment in kind in the rural sector. A very large proportion of all fixed investment would have been in buildings (45 percent) and vehicles (40 percent) and only a very small proportion (12 percent) in plant, machinery, and equipment. Most public investment has been financed by foreign grants and soft loans.

Because of the limited employment opportunities within Lesotho (total wage employment is estimated at just over 20,000), the Basotho have for many years sought employment in South Africa. Recent estimates are that about 175,000 men and 25,000 women are employed in South Africa on temporary contracts. The number of Basotho working in South Africa has increased by 6 to 7 percent a year over the last decade. Total earnings of Basotho workers in South Africa may now amount to more than R60 million a year (more than Lesotho's own GDP!), of which an estimated R15 million to R20 million is sent to Lesotho in one way or another. The migrant labor force is thus of critical economic significance for Lesotho.

At independence, the government inherited from the British administration a situation in which current expenditures were more than twice as high as current revenue. Up to fiscal 1968/69, British grants-in-aid financed about half of Lesotho's current budget. Since the 1969/70 period, Lesotho has received greatly increased revenue from the new customs agreement. The recurrent budget deficits decreased from about R6 million in the 1968/69 period to less than R2 million in the 1972/73 period, and in the 1973/74 period a surplus of R4 million is expected. The British government decreased its grants-in-aid correspondingly and stopped them altogether in the 1973/74 period.

The sharp decrease in budget deficits was also partly the result of a deliberate policy of Lesotho's government to reduce the country's dependence on British budget support as quickly as possible. Since the 1967/68 period, recurrent expenditures, which provide in most cases for only a minimal level of services, have not been allowed to increase in real terms. The low level of recurrent expenditures, however, has severely hampered the build-up of an adequate framework for planning and plan implementation and is therefore one of the reasons why government capital expenditure has remained at a low level of about R3 million a year. The availability of (mostly foreign) financial resources for the capital budget has not been a constraint.

C. Development Strategy and Future Prospects

The idea of development planning is quite new to Lesotho. Shortly after independence in 1966, the government established a Central Planning and Development Office; but, owing to serious initial staffing problems, it was not until 1971 that the Planning Office was able to publish the First Five-Year Development Plan 1970/71-1974/75 with the main objective to "lay the foundations for economic development and economic independence." The Plan's main development targets are as follows:

1. To achieve a marked increase in productivity in the main agricultural sector;
2. To promote as far as possible nonagricultural productive activities, putting special emphasis on small-scale indigenous industries;
3. To prepare for the full exploitation of the country's water and mineral resources;
4. To accomplish a radical and government-controlled development in education and post-school training related to the needs for economic and social advancement; and
5. To create 10,000 to 15,000 new employment opportunities, mainly in nonagricultural activities.

In order to achieve these goals, the Plan proposed a R28.8 million public sector capital expenditure program for the five-year period. In addition, the Plan estimated that during the Plan period about R25 million would be spent on the construction of the Malibamatso Water Export Project and that the Lesotho National Development Corporation would spend some R3 million from its own funds, mainly in the form of LNDC participation in foreign private industries to be attracted.

The emphasis the Plan places on the development of productive resources is basically sound; but, given the tentative character of many projects, the investment targets and development goals were quite unrealistic. In the first three years of the Plan, total government capital expenditures amounted to only 56 percent of the planned target and remained at about the same level as before the inception of the Plan. Moreover, relatively more than intended was spent on less productive government services and relatively less on productive sectors. One reason for this distortion is that projects in the government sector (office buildings and so forth) are easier to prepare and implement than those in other sectors.

It would be incorrect to state that the First Plan was too ambitious in the sense that finance would not have been available. Although no budgetary savings were anticipated over the Plan period, there are strong indications that foreign donors among them would have been willing to provide the necessary capital assistance, had there been a choice of projects ready for implementation. Nevertheless, the financial constraints have played a role in that the government's constant worries about the availability of local funds for development projects and for development-related recurrent expenditures, as well as the total dependence on foreign capital aid, have clearly frustrated project planning and implementation.

Since the inception of the First Plan, the government has made encouraging progress with identifying investment opportunities. A number of preinvestment studies have been undertaken which should help give the next Plan a solid foundation. The most important studies that have been completed or are currently under way include comprehensive transportation and tourism surveys, an industrial survey, a telecommunications development plan, a reconnaisance study for the development of electric power, and comprehensive surveys for the exploration of mineral resources. In the agricultural sector, recent schemes -- some of which are of a pilot nature -- are providing useful technical, economic, and sociological information which will greatly enhance the preparation of future projects. Last but not least, the government is taking important steps to improve the education system so as to gear it to the country's development needs.

In the past the most serious constraint to development has been the country's low absorptive capacity. In the future the substantially improved budgetary position should give the government much more leeway in planning. Recurrent revenue is likely to increase from R21 million in the 1973/74 period to about R45 million in the 1979/80 period. The government should use most of this increase to (a) build up its administrative framework for planning and plan implementation by strengthening the Central Planning Office and the planning units in the various ministries and (b) establish institutions outside the immediate government sphere, such as agricultural credit and marketing organizations as well as the development corporation, which is to cater to industrial and tourism development. More money, however, is not sufficient to provide better instruments for planning and plan execution. Lesotho is critically short of educated, skilled, and trained local manpower in all occupations and at all levels. Development of education, therefore, has high priority. But it will take considerable time before adequately educated and trained manpower will be available in sufficient numbers. In the meantime, there is an urgent need for more technical assistance.

If the government succeeds in overcoming the absorptive capacity constraints, it could aim at a capital expenditure program of some R85 million in the country's Second Five-Year Development Plan (1975/76-1979/80). Some R25 million local resources would be available (budget surpluses and local borrowing), and the rest -- R60 million -- is a realistic estimate of what foreign donors among them would be willing to make available in the five-year period. A capital investment program of this magnitude would imply an average annual increase of some 30 percent in real terms over the present level of capital expenditures.

In spite of the anticipated improvement in administrative capacity to prepare and implement development projects, the scarcity of natural resources and the difficult geographic position make economic prospects not particularly bright. Present and anticipated government programs in agriculture may lead to an increase in agricultural production of about 2.5

percent a year between now and the end of the decade. The employment effect of this, however, is not likely to be great, as it will be difficult to provide prospects of agricultural earnings that compare favorably with wages in South Africa. Nevertheless, agricultural development should have very high priority because (a) it is essential for erosion control; (b) it will, in any case, increase family incomes and provide better nutrition standards; and (c) it would secure a better basis to fall back on, should something go wrong with employment opportunities abroad.

Manufacturing industries and tourism offer the best employment opportunities within the country, but growth of these sectors depends largely on the readiness of foreign private enterprises to invest in Lesotho. The government itself is not planning any direct investment but is relying on favorable investment incentives and the activities of the Lesotho National Development Corporation to attract foreign investors. Assuming that a diamond mine will be established in the near future, that industrial production continues to grow at a rate of some 15 percent a year (the same as the estimated growth rate over the last three years), and assuming growth rates of 2.5 percent a year for agricultural production and 6 to 7 percent a year for the services sector (including government administration), GDP in real terms may grow at a rate of some 5 percent a year between now and the end of the decade.

Such a growth rate, however, is not likely to create new employment opportunities for more than about 12,000 persons by 1980, whereas Lesotho's labor force may increase by almost 75,000 persons. In the foreseeable future a large part of the labor force will have to continue to find jobs abroad. In these circumstances the government might wish to consider to give as much assistance to migrant workers as possible. A realistic emigration policy would not only imply market research into the most renumerative possibilities for migrant workers but also provision of technical training. Ideally, the government's education policy should, therefore, aim not only at overcoming domestic manpower constraints but also at improving the earning capacity of Lesotho's large migrant labor force.

I. LESOTHO'S CHALLENGE

Few developing countries faced such bleak economic prospects and were so ill-prepared as Lesotho when it gained independence in October 1966. In few countries in the world was economic independence more remote from political independence than in Lesotho. In spite of the fact that Lesotho is an enclave within highly industrialized South Africa and belongs with that country, Botswana, and Swaziland to the rand monetary area and the Southern African Customs Union, it was then virtually untouched by modern economic development. It was and still is, basically, a traditional subsistence peasant society. But rapid population growth resulting in extreme pressure on the land, deteriorating soil, and declining agricultural yields led to a situation in which the country was no longer able to produce enough food for its people. Many able-bodied men were forced from the land in search of means to support their families, but the only employment opportunities available were in neighboring South Africa. At present, an estimated 60 percent of the male labor force is away as migrant workers in South Africa.

At independence there was no economic infrastructure to speak of. Industries were virtually nonexistent. Whatever commerce there was, was largely in the hands of South African traders. The few commercial banks catered mainly for the small expatriate community. Education was dominated by foreign religious missions which had been quite active, giving Lesotho one of the highest literacy rates in Africa; but school curricula bore little relation to local conditions and to the development needs of the country. Former colonial rule was geared to administering the country and was not development oriented. At independence many colonial civil servants left. At the same time, the new government had to assume numerous new tasks for which few qualified Basotho were available. Government revenue was very low -- so low, in fact, that half of the recurrent budget and all of the capital budget had to be financed from foreign assistance, leaving the government little freedom in determining level and direction of expenditures.

There are several reasons why Lesotho has remained at such a low stage of social and economic development. One reason is that, until about 1950, the British government did not really attempt to introduce any development, expecting that the country would eventually be incorporated into South Africa and assuming that it would be more or less automatically developed as an indirect result of the strong expansionary forces in South Africa. But even when thoughts of incorporation were abandoned after the rise of the apartheid policies in South Africa, the British administration seems to have remained resigned to a low-level stagnation of Lesotho's rural economy. Apart from its eroding soil, Lesotho had few other known natural resources that could be developed; and the prevailing system of land tenure was seen to stand in the way of agricultural and industrial progress. In the five years before independence, capital expenditure was, on the average, less than R1 million a year, much of it for building up a local administration.

It was not until October 1965 -- one year before independence -- that the British government sent a mission (the Porter mission) to identify external assistance needs for a more vigorous socioeconomic development. This mission stressed development of infrastructure, agriculture, and education, recommending an increase in capital expenditure to R14 million over a five-year period. Lesotho's government, however, did not agree with either emphasis or level of the program recommended. It proposed a larger program (R20 million) with more investment in other productive sectors, particularly in manufacturing. But the British government did not accept either program. It considered Lesotho's requests for capital aid too high, in particular because they were not backed up by adequately prepared projects. The disagreement between the governments of Lesotho and Britain on the size and direction of development aid, together with the lack of a comprehensive development plan and the inability of many ministries to prepare projects, led until very recently to a rather haphazard pattern of capital expenditures with little coordination between various investment activities.

The government recognized the need for better development planning. Shortly after independence it established a Central Planning and Development Office, whose task it was to draft a first comprehensive development plan. Owing to serious initial staffing problems, however, it was not before the beginning of 1971 that the Planning Office was able to publish Lesotho's First Five-Year Development Plan 1970/71-1974/75 with the main objective "to lay the foundations for economic development and economic independence."

More in detail, the government's development targets are summarized as follows:

1. To attain an average annual rate of growth of gross domestic product of not less than 5 percent;

2. To achieve a marked increase in productivity in the agricultural sector;

3. To promote as far as possible nonagricultural productive activities, putting special emphasis on small-scale indigenous industries, and to secure the economic, legal, and institutional preconditions for a self-sustained development of these activities;

4. To prepare for the full exploitation of the country's water and mineral resources and, in particular, to carry out the first construction phase of the Malibamatso River Project;

5. To accomplish a radical and government-controlled development in education and post-school training related to the needs for economic and social advancement of the country;

6. To create 10,000 to 15,000 new employment opportunities, mainly in nonagricultural activities;

7. To bring about drastic changes in public administration so as to make its functioning more economical and its structure more development oriented;

8. To apply a realistic and systematic localization policy, primarily in the public sector, in accordance with the supply of qualified local personnel;

9. To effect a substantial improvement in social services in general and in health standards in particular;

10. To end the dependence of the government recurrent budget on external aid; and

11. To strengthen the economic relation and cooperation between Lesotho and other African countries and, in particular, with the countries of the Southern African Customs Union.

With an economy so dependent on export of labor to South Africa, a country with which Lesotho's political relations have always been very delicate, the emphasis on the development of the country's own productive resources is basically sound. But with a weak administration hampered by a lack of knowledge of the development potential of the country and with policy instruments normally available to an independent state limited by the country's association with the rand monetary area and the Southern African Customs Union, the government faces the tremendous challenge of achieving anything substantial in a situation where the previous administration seems to have accepted that all the odds are against it.

In order to achieve the growth and employment objectives, the Plan proposed a detailed five-year public sector capital expenditure program, which is summarized in Table 1.1. 1/

Table 1.1: SUMMARY OF THE PUBLIC INVESTMENT PROGRAM
1970/71-1974/75
(In thousand rand)

Agriculture	6,540
Industry	1,200
Mining	542
Commerce and tourism	513
Roads	6,502
Other economic infrastructure	1,713
Education	4,064
Water supply, sewerage, etc.	3,350
Other social infrastructure	1,166
General government services	3,212
Total	28,802

Source: Lesotho First Five-Year Development Plan, 1970/71-1974/75.

1/ For annual figures and more details, see Appendix Table 5.5.

In addition to this R28.8 million public investment program, the Plan estimated that during the Plan period about R25 million would be spent on the construction of the Malibamatso Water Project (see page 48), and that the Lesotho National Development Corporation (see page 49) would spend some R3 million from its own funds, mainly in the form of LNDC participation in foreign private industries to be attracted.

The published investment program did not consist of a program of clearly defined projects ready for implementation. Many of the ideas listed had not even reached the stage of preparation. To have expected better would have been unrealistic. The government knew that much needed to be done before a well-balanced investment program consistent with its development goals would be ready for implementation. It therefore called its plan a preparatory and exploratory plan.

One of the most important preparations to be undertaken before the government would be able to make the Plan work was the building of an administrative frame for planning and implementation. Besides a number of coordinating and review committees, the most crucial element of the planning framework was the setting up of sectoral programming units within the various executive ministries that would be responsible for the preparation and implementation of projects. Outside central government, several institutions (such as a development bank catering to small Basotho businessmen and farmers as well as a livestock marketing corporation) were to be established.

The Plan was exploratory in the sense that it was recognized that much investigation and exploration was still needed to determine the development potential and investment needs in the various sectors. Sponsored by a variety of multilateral and bilateral agencies, a number of surveys and preinvestment studies have been started; others are about to be undertaken, some of which are likely to lead to investment opportunities in the near future.

The First Plan period is now more than halfway through. Planned capital expenditures have seriously lagged behind targets, but this is hardly surprising given the state of preparation of the Plan at its inception. The Planning Office is now engaged in a critical review of the First Plan, both of its achievements and failures. With the lessons learned it intends to draw up a new Plan covering the period 1975/76-1979/80 which, with the help of recent or planned sector studies, will also have a more practical content than the present Plan. The purpose of this report is to help government with this exercise. In reviewing the economy, its institutions, and sectors, we intend to limit descriptions only to the extent that they are necessary to understand the workings of the economy and to concentrate instead on issues, bottlenecks, and their possible solutions.

II. THE SETTING

A. The Country

Lesotho is a small, landlocked country (11,716 square miles), entirely surrounded by the Republic of South Africa. About one-quarter of the country in the west and south is lowland country, varying in height from 5,000 to 6,000 feet. The rest of the country is mountainous with peaks that reach to over 11,000 feet. Only some 13 percent of the country is suited to crop cultivation. Most of the arable land is in the lowlands. The mountains are suitable only for grazing.

Lesotho's climate makes agriculture a risky business. Rainfall averages about 29 inches a year, which should normally be enough for farming and grazing. From time to time, however, extended droughts cause crop failures and loss of cattle. Averaged over a long period of time, droughts have occurred about one year in five; but in recent years there were severe droughts in 1969, 1970, and 1972. Even in years with good rains, it is necessary that enough rain falls during the short, critical period of about three weeks of field preparation. Most rain falls in the growing season; but heavy downpours and hailstorms are common, causing damage to soil and crops. In winter the weather in the mountains is too severe for grazing, and much of the cattle is then moved to the lowlands. Although frost also occurs in the lowlands, it is possible to grow winter crops.

Extreme pressure on the land, primitive methods of cultivation, and unchecked grazing have over the years led to acute erosion problems. About half of the cultivated areas and a not precisely known but substantial part of the mountain pastures are in various degrees affected by erosion. It is estimated that every year perhaps as much as one percent of the country's soil washes away and that on badly eroded land, if nothing is done, crop yields would fall steadily at a rate of about 5 percent a year.

Lesotho's erosion problems were recognized long ago, and the technical answers to solve them are there. Since the mid-1930s the Ministry of Agriculture has been carrying out a soil conservation program; but, with limited funds, not nearly enough could be achieved. Also and more seriously, this program was not tied in with any agricultural programs. Bad farming practices continued, which led to further erosion. Only recently, newly evolving insights as to how to develop subsistence farming within existing systems of traditional land tenure and with full involvement of the people hold out hope that what remains of Lesotho's soil can be saved.

Apart from its eroding soil, Lesotho has few other known natural resources. One abundant natural asset, which is not being tapped yet, is water in the mountains. A feasibility study has been prepared for a project to export large quantities of water to South Africa (see page 48). The potential for irrigation has not been investigated systematically, but what studies there are suggest that it is limited.

So far, mining has been confined to some small-scale diamond digging. A mineral survey is being carried out by UNDP, and a few large companies have prospected for diamonds. One large company has decided to establish a medium-size diamond mine. Oil prospecting is presently being undertaken.

Another natural asset still largely untapped is Lesotho's beautiful mountain scenery. Several foreign tourist enterprises have expressed an interest in building holiday resorts in the mountains. A team of consultants sponsored by the Commonwealth Secretariat has recently brought out a report on the country's tourism potential.

B. Human Resources

Owing to the lack of reliable data on labor movements across the border, the size of Lesotho's de jure population is not precisely known. In 1966, the latest census year, the country had a resident population of 852,000 persons. In addition, 117,000 people were reported to be temporarily absent, most of them employed in South Africa. The latter figure, however, is thought to be too low, as it would not include those considered to be illegally in South Africa. Fragmentary information on employment of Basotho in South Africa suggests a figure of at least 150,000 absentees in 1966, which would mean a total de jure population of one million in 1966. Of the total resident population in 1966, only about 2,300 were non-Africans -- mainly government servants, traders, teachers, and missionaries.

According to previous censuses, Lesotho's resident population grew at an average annual rate of only 0.7 percent between 1936 and 1956, but the rate of increase was much higher between 1956 and 1966 -- namely, 2.9 percent a year. Although the results of earlier censuses should be used with caution, the difference in growth rates in the two periods is striking. It seems evident that in the earlier period a substantial portion of Lesotho's population increase -- perhaps as much as 150,000 people in total -- was permanently absorbed by South Africa. The much faster population growth between 1956 and 1966 can partly be explained by the fact that since the early 1950s movements of migrant labor have increasingly become subject to South African control, which made permanent Basotho settlement in South Africa difficult.

There are no reliable estimates of birth and death rates. The United Nations uses an estimate of 2 percent. A recent study in Lesotho 1/ based on a sample of rural households in the 1967/68 period suggests a natural rate of increase of 2.2 percent. Applying this rate to the 1966 census data and assuming that the number of absentees has increased to some 200,000 at present (see page 18), Lesotho's African population may be estimated to have grown between 1966 and 1973 as given in Table 2.1.

1/ Report on the Demographic Component of the Rural Household Consumption and Expenditure Survey 1967-1968, Bureau of Statistics, May 1973.

Table 2.1: AFRICAN POPULATION, 1966 and 1973
(In thousands)

	1966	1973	Annual rate of increase
De jure population	1,000	1,165	2.2%
Of which			
Absent from Lesotho	150	200	4.3%
De facto population	850	965	1.8%

Source: Mission estimates.

The population growth has brought increasing pressure on the limited land resources. The 1970 agricultural census 2/ reveals how seriously the situation has deteriorated over the last two decades. The number of people per acre of arable land increased from 0.7 to 1.2 between 1950 and 1970. Over the same period the average family holding of cropland decreased from 6.2 acres to 4.9 acres. In 1950, 7 percent of the rural households had no land at all; by 1970 this percentage had increased to 13.

Lesotho has a healthy climate, and tropical diseases are few and uncommon. Nevertheless, the general health standard of the people is not good. Chronic undernourishment and malnutrition are responsible for a low resistance to such diseases as tuberculosis, typhoid, and gastroenteritis. A nutritional survey conducted by the World Health Organization between 1956 and 1960 brought to light that at that time no less than 85 percent of the children below the age of eight were retarded in their physical development because of hunger and malnutrition. There are no later surveys; but, as a result of several food aid programs, school feeding programs, and mother and child care programs, the situation is likely to have improved.

With the increasing shortage of land and limited employment opportunities outside agriculture, there is a strong case for a population policy in Lesotho. In normal circumstances, a vigorous emigration policy would be appropriate for a country with obviously too many people and too few means to support them. Because of South Africa's racial policies, however, the government is understandably hesitant to encourage emigration to that country. In any case, present South African immigration laws prohibit permanent settlement of foreign African laborers. But in view of the fact that, in spite of all development effort, only a relatively small proportion of the increase in the labor force is likely to be absorbed by Lesotho's own economy (see page 67), it would appear advisable for the government to assume a more active role in labor migration in order to provide prospective Basotho migrant workers with as much guidance and assistance as possible. Another possibility of a population policy would be some form of official support to family planning. At the moment, the government feels that it would be

2/ 1970 Census of Agriculture Report, Bureau of Statistics, December 1972.

difficult for social and religious reasons to give open support; but, on the other hand, the government is not opposed to it. On a private basis, the Lesotho Family Planning Association (sponsored by the International Planned Parenthood Federation) operates family planning clinics which are reported to have some success; and government doctors are allowed to provide services, making use of official facilities, if people ask for them.

C. Land Tenure: An Insurmountable Obstacle?

A succession of overseas economic missions, the last one as late as 1965, 3/ have without exception stated categorically that the traditional system of land tenure is quite unsuited to modern economic development and that it was a man-made obstacle whose removal was a precondition for economic growth. But is this so? What is insufficiently recognized is that Lesotho's land tenure system has never been a rigid system; on the contrary, it has molded itself continuously to changing circumstances and needs as felt by the people. The type of modern agricultural development advocated, however, was usually patterned after European farming and cattle ranching practices, which were so revolutionary and alien to Lesotho's rural subsistence society that people were simply put off.

The concept underlying the land tenure system is that land is a national and social asset to be enjoyed by the Basotho nation as a whole. The authorities have never permitted alienation of land and rural settlement by foreigners. The King holds the land in trust for the nation. He controls the exploitation and distribution of land; but he has delegated much of his authority to his subordinates, the chiefs, subchiefs, and village headmen. His subordinates hand out land rights to the people, rights which have always been less than full ownership or freehold.

Lesotho law draws a distinction between urban and rural land. In urban areas the chiefs grant occupancy rights for urban living. Occupancy rights have in the past also been granted to foreigners, mainly to missions for their churches, schools, and clinics and to traders for their shops and stores. In rural areas the chiefs allocate to heads of families arable land according to the families' subsistence needs. Animals may be grazed on the communal mountain pastures and also on the arable land which, after the harvest, reverts to communal use. This system was adequate for a traditional agricultural society where there were few additional needs to be satisfied beyond pure subsistence and where land was relatively abundant. Since this was the type of society that people had known for a long time, little need for changing the system was felt.

The present system has also its good sides. Had Lesotho had a system of transferable landownership, land would undoubtedly have accumulated in the hands of a few -- first of all, in the hands of foreign settlers

---

3/ The British Ministry of Overseas Development Economic Survey Mission (the Porter mission).

(nearby Swaziland is a case in point where, at independence, more than half of the land was owned by foreigners) but also in the hands of more enterprising Basotho farmers. This would presumably have led to higher agricultural productivity, but it would also have created an enormous landless proletariat. The 1970 agricultural census reveals that at present no great inequities in the distribution of land exist. The average landholding is 4.9 acres. Most individual holdings vary from 2 to 15 acres, but there is a strong positive correlation between size of holding and family size. The land allotted to a family is usually scattered over two or three plots to achieve a just distribution among families of good and bad land.

The rapid population growth in the last decades and the resulting pressure on the land call now for a dramatic increase in agricultural producitivity. The size of family holdings has decreased to the point that they provide not nearly enough food for the families' subsistence. The common pastures in the mountains were long seen as inexhaustible and limitless, but more people also brought more cattle. This, together with the traditional preference of the Basotho for quantity rather than quality, has led to serious overstocking, which is a major cause of soil erosion. Under the traditional system pastures are not allowed to be fenced, which makes proper pasture management virtually impossible. Uncontrolled breeding has caused a steady decline in the quality of livestock.

Until very recently modern agricultural development was not even attempted by foreign donors because the land tenure system was seen to stand in the way of all progress. The lack of security of tenure made the farmer reluctant to make any permanent land improvements, and the absence of negotiable title to the land meant that farmers had no security to offer for credit for the purchase of implements, seed, fertilizer, and so forth. All this led to a vicious circle: in the absence of agricultural development schemes, it was never demonstrated to the people that anything worthwhile could be achieved on their land; therefore, people saw no need for changes.

In the First Five-Year Development Plan, it was recognized that the land tenure system is an obstacle to transforming Lesotho's subsistence society into an agricultural cash economy along Western lines. But land tenure being a sensitive issue, no changes were proposed or even discussed. Instead, the Plan states as one of its targets "to investigate the suitability of mechanization methods under the country's social and ecological conditions, and to test the compatibility of the land tenure system with a rapid expansion of agricultural productivity." To this end, a 5,000-acre pilot agricultural scheme was started in 1970, executed by FAO and financed by UNDP and the Lesotho government. Encouraging findings with respect to land tenure so far are, first, that the lack of security of tenure and the inability to use land as a security for credit are, at present, less of an obstacle than previously believed; and, second and more important, that by involving chiefs and people from the very outset and showing them that agricultural productivity can, indeed, be increased dramatically on their land, people are prepared to speed up the slow evolution of tenurial concepts, once they are convinced that changes are to their benefit.

Changes in tenurial concepts have been most pronounced with respect to urban land; and, since they may eventually have some effect on the attitude towards rural land, we will discuss them first. In contrast to expatriate traders who apparently considered the occupancy rights granted by chiefs sufficiently secure to establish themselves in Lesotho, foreign industrial investors were deterred by the impossibility of obtaining land as freehold or on a long lease. The government, realizing this and wanting to make a beginning with industrial development, established in 1963 the Basutoland Factory Estates Development Company (BAFED). BAFED was granted a fifty-year lease on a site in Maseru to be developed into an industrial estate. BAFED was, thus, able to pass on to prospective industrial investors reasonable security of tenure. Owing to organizational difficulties, however, BAFED was not very successful. In 1967 it was reorganized and absorbed by the government-owned Lesotho National Development Corporation (LNDC), to which BAFED's lease was transferred for an indefinite period. LNDC has been successful in attracting a number of industries and has acquired a second area for industrial development. LNDC has gradually moved into other areas where traditional land rights interfered with modern development. Acting as an intermediary between the King and investors, it has acquired long-term leases for corporate housing and the building of hotels. Also, according to legislation introduced in 1967, LNDC represents the nation with respect to mineral rights and is entitled to grant prospecting rights and concessions to companies and individuals.

The banks do not consider the individual occupancy rights for urban living a sufficient collateral for the granting of mortgage loans. This has severely hampered housing development in Lesotho. Some solution was provided by the Deeds Registry Act of 1968, by which the Law Office may register urban sites and furnish "Certificates of Registered Title." Although these titles are less than transferable leaseholds, it became possible to obtain mortgage loans on immobilities from local banks. But, since these banks are in the first place commercial banks not geared to providing long-term loans, business remained limited. Building societies operating in Lesotho are all subsidiaries of South African firms. They have been collecting savings deposits in Lesotho but have not yet invested there. According to South African law, they were unable to do so before Lesotho's government had enacted legislation providing for the possibility of transferable leasehold. Such legislation was passed in November 1973.

In rural areas with their more conservative population, the evolution of tenurial concepts will undoubtedly be much slower. A more rapid evolution, however, does not seem to be very urgent because the traditional occupancy rights to rural land do already give the farmer a reasonable security of tenure. The holder has always had the right of occupation and use of land for his lifetime, and he may not be deprived of his land without good reason. It is true that the reasons for dispossession are vaguely defined. In the past they left much room for arbitrary interpretation and action by the chiefs. In recent times, however, it has become increasingly difficult for chiefs to dispossess farmers of their holdings. In case of a dispute, the farmer can bring his case before the court. Also, quite spontaneously, village development committees have been emerging which, in practice, exert a large measure of control over the chiefs. The government intends to encourage the formation of these committees and plans to enact legislation which would give them a formal status. Together with this, it would appear desirable to achieve a formal codification of possible reasons for dispossession of land, reasons which should be easy for farmers to understand and normally within their power to avoid.

Also, the traditional tenurial concepts with respect to land use have gradually changed under the influence of new economic circumstances. Traditionally after the harvest the individual holdings for the cultivation of crops were turned into communal grazing land. With the introduction of winter crops, it has become generally accepted, however, that the farmer who wants to keep his land under cultivation has the right to fence his land to keep out roaming cattle. One of the greatest obstacles to better land-use planning, however, is the tremendous fragmentation of cropland. Nevertheless, there are already instances of progressive chiefs who have allowed pooling of individual landholdings by farmers who wanted to form cooperatives. Changing the attitude towards communal grazing on the mountain pasture seems to be more difficult. The government is painfully aware that, in order to check erosion, drastic changes are called for. Empowered by the Land Husbandry Act of 1969, the government is now drafting regulations which will make fencing of mountain pastures and rotational grazing possible. The beneficial effects of this on pastures and cattle have already been demonstrated in a few instances, and the government expects that this will lead to a ready acceptance by both chiefs and cattle owners of the grazing regulations to be introduced.

D. Economic Ties with South Africa

Together with South Africa, Botswana, and Swaziland, Lesotho belongs to the rand currency area and the Southern African Customs Union. With certain flaws to be discussed below, there is, in principle, a free movement of goods and funds within the area. This situation has both advantages and disadvantages for the three small countries. An obvious advantage is the free access that Lesotho's industries have to a large market with a great purchasing power. For many of its agricultural exports, Lesotho benefits from the high support prices paid to South African producers. Furthermore, Lesotho is able to draw on the foreign exchange reserves of South Africa. In devising development projects for foreign financing, Lesotho is, therefore, relieved of the worry that such projects -- directly or indirectly -- will have to earn foreign exchange to service debts. The disadvantages of the arrangements are mainly that they severely limit the set of policy instruments normally available to independent countries. Although in theory the arrangements provide for consultation on policy matters among the participating countries, in practice it has been the strongest member, South Africa, who has determined the policies related to foreign exchange, exchange rates, monetary matters, and levels of customs, excise, and sales taxes. These policies are generally determined in the best interest of the three smaller countries.

South Africa's currency, the rand, is at present used as legal tender in Lesotho without any formal agreements between the governments concerned and without any official institutional arrangements. Thus, Lesotho has no central bank of its own. Until recently most commercial banking functions were performed by two foreign banking groups -- the Standard Bank

Limited and Barclays Bank International Ltd. -- which are incorporated in the United Kingdom but follow practices similar to those of their regional head offices in South Africa.

Lesotho is presently engaged in discussions with South Africa with a view to negotiating a formal monetary agreement. Most of the unwritten arrangements which have been working adequately are expected to be institutionalized. Improvements that the government of Lesotho is aiming at include, inter alia, (a) a share in the revenue from the investments backing the currency in circulation, (b) a formalized provision for mutual consultation on monetary policies, (c) formalized guaranteed access to foreign exchange, and (d) finding ways by which Lesotho can make more use of rand area's capital and money markets located in South Africa. In 1969 South Africa formally made its capital market facilities available to the government of Lesotho, but there is no provision yet for short-term borrowing in the South African money markets.

Under the Customs Union, which has been in existence since 1910, all customs as well as excise and sales duties collected in the customs area are paid into a common revenue pool administered by South Africa. Up to 1969 the South African government returned annually a fixed share -- 1.31 percent -- to its three partners. Until 1965 Lesotho's share in the total pool had remained unchanged at 0.89 percent. In 1965, however, the British government reallocated the 1.31 percent total share among three countries to bring their allocations more in line with the relative value of their imports. Since over the years Lesotho's imports had increased much less than those of Botswana and Swaziland, Lesotho's share was then decreased to 0.47 percent.

The allocation of 1.31 percent of the total pool to the three countries was based on trade statistics for the period 1906-1908. Once the countries received independence, their governments argued that they were receiving much too small a share in the revenue pool. In 1969 a new Customs Union Agreement was concluded between South Africa, Botswana, Lesotho, and Swaziland. The new agreement is a great improvement for the three small countries. Redistribution of the common pool is now determined by the countries' actual annual share of imports as well as by production and consumption of excisable and dutiable goods. The pro rata share of the three countries is multiplied by a factor 1.42, which is intended to represent conpensation by South Africa to its three partners for certain disadvantages of belonging to a customs union with a more developed partner. Among these disadvantages are the natural tendency towards polarization of industrial development in areas which are already industrially advanced, all of which are in South Africa; the price-raising effects of tariffs primarily designed to protect South African industries; and the loss of certain fiscal discretion. The new arrangements, together with an improved reporting of imports, provide Lesotho with substantially increased revenues (see page 25).

Also, in other respects the new customs agreement is an improvement over the old one. As an exception to the rule of "free trade" in the customs area, the three smaller countries will, for the first time, be able to give their industries some degree of protection from competition originating in the other countries of the customs area. For a maximum of eight years,

Botswana, Lesotho, or Swaziland may, after appropriate consultations, impose additional duties to protect new industries -- but only insofar as these industries produce for their own domestic markets. In addition, the three small countries may specify "industries of major importance" to their economies, in which case South Africa undertakes not to reduce customs duties on competing imports from outside the customs area or, if necessary, to give sympathetic consideration to proposals by the small countries to increase common duties. In these cases South Africa has undertaken to apply the same norms as are used in considering requests for protection from South African industries. Also, under the new agreement the member countries may enter into individual trade agreements with countries outside the customs area, provided that tariff concessions granted shall apply only to imports used in the member country concerned.

Botswana, Lesotho, and Swaziland have not yet availed themselves of the possibility of imposing additional duties to protect infant industries. Because of the small size of their economies, the possibilities for industries producing solely for the domestic market are certainly not great. In fact, the main opportunity which the customs agreement offers to industrial development in the three countries is access to the large market of the area as a whole. In this respect, the customs agreement offers no means that would protect emerging industries in the small countries against competition from well-established, efficient, and large-scale production units in South Africa. What is more, existing administrative and cartel arrangements in South Africa have, in spite of the principle of a free flow of goods, acted as a deterrent to the establishment of large-scale industries in the three small countries. In the light of these problems, Botswana, Lesotho, and Swaziland need to keep the customs union arrangements and South African trading practices under constant scrutiny in order to identify defects and to take steps to protect their interests.

Lesotho's economic ties to South Africa go far beyond the monetary and customs area arrangements. South Africa is the main outlet for Lesotho's exports. Only few of the merchandise exports are consumed in South Africa; three of the four most important export commodities -- wool, mohair, and diamonds -- are reexported overseas. Trade statistics do not provide a country-by-country breakdown of merchandise imports, but imports from outside South Africa are probably small. For its outward communications, Lesotho depends on South African rail, air, and telecommunication services. Most of the electricity used in Lesotho is generated in South Africa. Most industries have been developed through South African investment. Lesotho's young tourist industry depends nearly entirely on the South African market. Also, most of the service industries in Lesotho are South African owned. South African companies and individuals dominate insurance, foreign trade, and the domestic wholesale and retail business. Traditionally, South Africa has provided employment to a large portion of Lesotho's labor force. At present, about 60 percent of the male labor force and about 10 percent of the female labor force are working in South Africa. There is no doubt that Lesotho derives significant benefits from its rich neighbor. But on the other hand, it is equally clear that the maneuverability of the government in its economic policies is de facto severely hampered by the country's close ties to South Africa. The government, therefore, is anxious to diversify Lesotho's international relations. It is increasingly seeking more financial and technical assistance from other countries and multilateral agencies; it is attempting to attract more private investment from overseas; and it is presently negotiating some form of association with the European Economic Community.

III. TRENDS IN THE ECONOMY AS A WHOLE

A. Summary of Trends

Economic indicators for Lesotho are scarce and unreliable. The government's own budget statistics are the only reliable information available. Production statistics are virtually nonexistent. Whatever indicators there are, however, all point to poverty and stagnation over a long period of time, reflecting the country's poor natural resources and lack of development in the past. Agricultural censuses held in 1950, 1960, and 1970 suggest a steady decline in crop production over the last two decades. Livestock production might have remained more or less stable. Manufacturing output is estimated to have tripled since 1967, but its contribution to GDP is still insignificant. It would not be unrealistic to assume that in real terms GDP per capita has fallen slightly over the last decade or so. This decrease has most likely been compensated by an increase in remittances from migrant workers. Per capita GNP, therefore, may have remained more or less stable at about US$100 at current exchange rates and prices.

B. National Accounts

Given the lack of economic information, it is obviously very difficult to compile a realistic set of national accounts. The various estimates made in the past show large annual fluctuations, invariably reflecting different methodologies used by different experts. Only recently has the Bureau of Statistics started to compile national accounts on a year-by-year comparable basis. Some preliminary estimates covering the period 1966/67-1970/71 were made available to the mission; but, because of some obvious inconsistencies and omissions, they do not yet provide a basis for serious analysis. The national account data given in the following paragraphs serve merely as a rough illustration of the economic framework and should be viewed with great caution.

The rural sector, with a contribution of some 60 percent, is by far the largest sector. Agriculture proper contributes about 45 percent of GDP. About two-thirds of this is derived from crop cultivation, the rest from livestock. About one-third of all agricultural output enters the monetized sector. The other productive sectors are all very small. In percentage terms, output of the manufacturing and construction sectors increased fast between the 1966/67 and 1970/71 periods -- an increase which has continued after the 1970/71 period -- but this reflects the very small base in the 1966/67 period. In absolute terms the contribution of these sectors to GDP is still insignificant. The figures in Table 3.1 are in current prices. The totals for GDP at factor cost suggest an increase of 2 percent a year between the 1966/67 and 1970/71 periods. But assuming a general price increase of 3 percent a year and an annual growth of the de facto population of 1.8 percent, real per capita GDP would have decreased by some 2.5 percent a year over the same period.

Table 3.1: INDUSTRIAL ORIGIN OF GDP AT FACTOR COST, 1966/67 AND 1970/71

	1966/67		1970/71	
	Million rand	Percent of total	Million rand	Percent of total
Rural sector	25.1	63.9	25.6	60.2
Agriculture	18.9	48.1	19.0	44.8
Home industries	0.5	1.2	0.5	1.2
Construction	0.5	1.4	0.6	1.4
Ownership of dwellings	4.8	12.3	5.2	12.1
Other services	0.4	0.9	0.3	0.7
Other sectors	14.1	36.1	16.9	39.8
Productive sectors	1.4	3.6	2.3	5.4
Mining, quarrying	0.7	1.8	0.7	1.7
Manufacturing	0.3	0.8	0.7	1.7
Water, electricity	0.1	0.3	0.3	0.6
Construction	0.3	0.7	0.6	1.3
Service sectors	12.7	32.5	14.6	34.4
Commerce, catering, transport, communications	5.5	14.0	5.8	13.6
Financial and professional services	0.4	1.1	0.5	2.8
Ownership of dwellings	1.0	2.6	1.2	2.8
Community services, including government administration	5.4	13.8	6.8	16.0
Other services	0.4	0.9	0.3	0.8
Total	39.2	100.0	42.5	100.0

Source: Bureau of Statistics and mission estimates.

GDP at market prices was estimated at R47.5 million; but, because of substantial remittances by Basotho working in South Africa, GNP at market prices is higher. The precise amount of remittances is not known. The registered transfers, as reported by the South African mines and the post office, were R4.7 million in 1970; but actual transfers are most likely much higher. According to recent estimates, total earnings of Basotho workers in South Africa may have amounted to about R60 million in 1970 (more than Lesotho's own GDP!), of which perhaps 25 percent is sent to Lesotho in one way or another. The number of Basotho working in South Africa may have increased by more than 40 percent over the last six years (see page 18). Their remittances have undoubtedly made a substantial contribution to the development of the monetized sector of Lesotho's economy. With the recent 50 percent increase in wages for lower-paid mine workers in South Africa, the inflow of remittances will increase even more sharply.

Gross fixed investment was estimated at R5 million in the 1970/71 period (just over 10 percent of GDP). About half of this would have been investment by the government and public enterprises; and the rest represents investment by private enterprises, missions, as well as investment in kind in the rural sector. A very large proportion of fixed investment would have been in buildings (45 percent) and vehicles (40 percent) with only a very small proportion (12 percent) in plant, machinery, and equipment (Appendix Table 2.2). Most of the public investment was financed by foreign grants and loans. Little is known about the way private investments were financed. The figures in Table 3.2 suggest a negative savings rate in the 1970/71 period. Total consumption expenditures would have exceeded gross national product by R6.5 million. The gap between gross national product and total domestic expenditure (R9 million) would have been bridged by British budget and capital grants (R4 million), some other official long-term capital inflow (R1 million), private capital inflow (R2 to R3 million), and for the rest by private remittances, a large part by missions and voluntary agencies.

Table 3.2: NATIONAL ACCOUNTS: ORIGIN AND USE OF RESOURCES, 1970/71

	Million rand
Origin	
GDP at factor cost	42.5
Indirect taxes less subsidies	5.0
GDP at market prices	47.5
Net factor income from abroad	14.5
GNP at market prices	62.0
Import of goods and services	35.5
Factor income paid abroad	0.5
Total	98.0
Use	
Private consumption	55.5
Public consumption	10.0
Gross fixed capital formation	5.0
Change in stocks	0.5
Domestic expenditure	71.0
Exports of goods and services	12.0
Factor income from abroad	15.0
Total	98.0

Source: Bureau of Statistics and mission estimates.

Because of sharply increased revenue from the Customs Union, the situation with respect to national savings should have become much more favorable in recent years. The government's recurrent budget showed a deficit of R3 million in the 1970/71 period but shows a surplus of about R4 million in the 1973/74 period.

C. Employment

Comprehensive statistics on size, distribution, and growth of Lesotho's labor force are not available. Extrapolating information gathered through the 1966 population census, the total labor force in 1973 may be estimated at some 450,000 persons -- 290,000 men and 160,000 women. Lesotho's economy is unable to absorb this labor force. In mid-1973 more than 110,000 Basotho men were registered as employed in South African mines on six- to twelve-month contracts. In addition, a substantial number of men, variously estimated between 40,000 and 90,000 (about 65,000) are in other temporary employment in South Africa on farms, in commerce and industry, and with South African Railways. This means that at present between 50 and 70 percent (about 60 percent) of Lesotho's active male labor force is employed in South Africa. The migrant female labor force is estimated at 25,000 persons, most of them working in domestic services. Statistics on Lesotho's present resident labor force are scarce. Rough estimates indicate that 21,000 persons (16,000 men and 5,000 women) find wage employment within Lesotho. The government employs about 7,500 of them. About 3,000 to 3,500 persons are employed in manufacturing, construction, public utilities, and tourism. The rest would be employed in the services sector.

Over the last six years, the number of Basotho men employed by South African mines has increased by 40,000 or by 7.5 to 8 percent a year on the average. Over the same period, wage employment for men within Lesotho might have increased by some 2,000 jobs, most of them provided by LNDC-sponsored companies (see page 49). Assuming that Lesotho's labor force grows at the same rate as the de jure population (2.2 percent a year) and that employment for Basotho men in South Africa outside the mines has increased by another 10,000, the following picture of the development of Lesotho's male labor force may be derived from Table 3.3.

Table 3.3: BASOTHO MALE LABOR FORCE, 1967 AND 1973
(Number of persons)

	1967	1973	Change
Total labor force	255,000	290,000	+35,000
Employed in South Africa	125,000	175,000	+50,000
Wage employment within Lesotho	14,000	16,000	+ 2,000
Available for work in the traditional sector	116,000	99,000	-17,000

Source: Mission estimates.

Laborers for the South African mines are recruited by a number of South African organizations operating in Lesotho. Basotho laborers, who specialize in shaft sinking, have so far been much in demand. But the Lesotho government can, of course, never be sure that this will remain so. Over the past decade total African employment in the South African mines has increased by 6.7 percent a year. The share of Basotho labor in total African labor in the South African mines increased from 11 percent in 1963 to 19 percent in 1973 (Table 3.4).

Table 3.4: AFRICAN MINE LABOR IN SOUTH AFRICA, 1963 AND 1973
(Number of persons)

	Total	Basotho
1963	523,000	58,000
1973	590,000	111,000

Source: South African Reserve Bank, quarterly bulletins, Lesotho Department of Labor.

The Lesotho government has doubts as to whether South Africa wishes to increase its dependence on foreign labor much further. It is also afraid that, with increasing mechanization in the mines, the employment opportunities for Basotho will level off. The tendency towards further mechanization will undoubtedly receive a powerful spur from the 50 percent increase in wages paid for lower-paid mine labor introduced in the beginning of 1973. The wage increases will also make mine labor more attractive to South Africa's own African labor force.

In its First Five-Year Development Plan, the government, therefore, laid a strong emphasis on employment creation within Lesotho. The target for the Five-Year Plan period was 10,000 to 15,000 new jobs or, on the average, 2,000 to 3,000 a year, mainly in nonagricultural activities. In terms of need, this is a modest goal. Table 3.3 illustrates that for men alone an annual increase in nonagricultural jobs of almost 9,000 would have been needed to absorb the natural increase in the labor force as well as men leaving the land. But, compared to the number of Basotho presently employed outside the agricultural sector in Lesotho, the target of creating 2,000 to 3,000 new jobs a year has been achieved so far.

The government plans to reach its employment target by promoting much more vigouously than before such sectors as manufacturing and tourism (see sections on Sectors). If past experience is a guide, however, an increase in employment of 2,000 to 3,000 new jobs a year is not even enough to absorb the number of men leaving the land (Table 3.3). Agricultural development designed in such a way that it arrests and eventually reserves the flow of men leaving the land should, therefore, have very high priority. The pull of the South African labor market, however, poses two peculiar problems with respect to agricultural development. First, the able-bodied men who are available between contracts are usually not very interested in agricultural work; and much of the farm labor is done by women, children and old men.

A serious impediment in agriculture is that there is almost no permanent core of male labor. Second, in order to compete with wages in South Africa, cash income from farms should be increased to some R300 a year. The average cash income on traditional farms is at present no more than about R20 a year. In the Leribe agricultural pilot scheme (see page 43), which has been operating for three years, it has been demonstrated that cash income from farms (over subsistence needs) can easily be doubled; but, on the other hand, there is no evidence yet that because of this, rather than seeking employment in South Africa, men have preferred to stay on the farms in Lesotho.

D. Wages

The Department of Labor (part of the Ministry of Finance) is responsible for labor relations in the private sector. However, whatever labor legislation exists -- most of it with respect to working conditions -- is hardly enforced. Wage levels in Lesotho in both the private and public sectors have generally remained stable since 1964, but pressures for increases have been mounting. Both bank employees and teachers obtained substantial wage increases in 1972. In 1973 the government appointed a Wage Advisory Board, which is to make recommendations with respect to minimum wage legislation. In devising a wage policy, however, the government is caught in a difficult dilemma. On the one hand, it recognizes that, in order not to endanger the competitiveness of investment in labor-intensive industries, wage levels cannot be pushed up too far. On the other hand, wages in Lesotho should offer a sufficiently attractive alternative to wages in South Africa. In particular, for technically skilled labor the wage differential between Lesotho and South Africa is large. The demand for such labor in South Africa is great, and there has been a troublesome drain on Lesotho's scarse skilled manpower.

Published information on wage levels in the private industry is scanty. Interviews with the private sector revealed the following picture. In the foreign-owned private industries, casual laborers are paid R15 a month. This is the same as the government pays its casual laborers, and this level is unofficially regarded as the minimum wage. Unskilled but trained laborers earn from R25 to R30 a month in private industries. Skilled workers earn from R40 to R50 a month. In the South African mines wages run from some R20 a month for completely untrained and unskilled laborers ("novices") to R40 a month for trained workers. In addition, the mines provide free food and lodging.

In the civil service, salary scales have remained unchanged since October 1964. Annual salaries of professionals and top administrative personnel range from about R2,000 to R6,200. In lower clerical and technical assistance scales, however, annual salaries are not more than R320 to R1,400. Agricultural extension workers, for instance, belong to this category; and their salaries range from R520 to R1,100. Housing for civil servants is subsidized, and rents vary with the type of house and the salary scale from R12 to R42 a month. There are a substantial number of expatriates in the middle and higher levels of the civil service, and their salaries are topped up by the agencies by whom they are sponsored. The government inherited the civil service salary structure from the British administration, and it recognizes that the salaries for top functions are completely out of line with incomes in the rest of the economy and with what the country can afford. It has, therefore, been a deliberate government policy to keep salaries frozen at their 1964 levels. Assuming that the South African cost-of-living index gives a fair approximation of price developments in Lesotho, civil service salaries decreased by some 33 percent in real terms between 1964 and 1973.

E. Income Distribution

The 1970 Census of Agriculture (report published in December 1972) and the 1972/73 Urban Household Budget Survey (report published in October 1973) provide valuable material on which a reliable analysis of income distribution can be based. The results show a remarkable equality of incomes in Lesotho (Table 3.5).

The income inequality is most pronounced among the urban population with only one percent of total urban income earned by the lower 5 percent and with 26 percent of the income earned by the highest 5 percent. Such distribution patterns, however, are not unusual in a situation with a relatively large class of expatriates and civil servants and with a very small industrial sector. As the urban population amounts to no more than 4 percent of the total population, the influence of the inequality within the urban class on the income distribution pattern of the population as a whole is not large.

The remarkably even distribution of incomes of the rural population is the result of two factors. First, the distribution of productive assets is quite even. The lowest 20 percent own 14 percent of the cattle and hold 8 percent of the arable land. The highest 20 percent own 26 percent of the cattle and hold 37 percent of the arable land. This is in sharp contrast with, for instance, Botswana, where the lowest 20 percent own only one percent of the cattle and hold 3 percent of the arable land and where the highest 20 percent own 70 percent of the cattle and hold 50 percent of the arable land. Second, the incidence of migrant labor is higher among poorer families than among the richer. Therefore, the farm incomes of the poorer rural households are supplemented by income from migrant labor to a greater extent than those of the relatively richer households. In turn, the latter factor may partly explain the even distribution of cattle ownership, as monetary savings in Lesotho are often used to buy more cattle. The ultimate result is that the lowest 20 percent of the rural population earn about 16 percent of total income and the highest 20 percent earn 26 percent of total income, a degree of equality which is not matched in any other country known to the mission. It should, however, be borne in mind that this is achieved at a higher social cost (more disruption of family life, more exposure to apartheid policies) for the poorer households. Regional differences in rural incomes are discussed on pages 39-40.

Table 3.5: **DISTRIBUTION OF WEALTH AND INCOME**

DISTRIBUTION OF WEALTH
Rural population

Percent owned, respectively held by	Cattle	Arable land
Lowest 5%	3	2
Lowest 20%	14	8
Lowest 40%	31	21
Highest 40%	48	61
Highest 20%	26	37
Highest 5%	9	11

DISTRIBUTION OF INCOME
Rural population

Percent earned by	Farm income	Total income
Lowest 5%	2	4
Lowest 20%	9	16
Lowest 40%	22	33
Highest 40%	58	47
Highest 20%	33	26
Highest 5%	11	8

Urban population

Percent earned by	Total urban class	Excluding expatriates
Lowest 5%	1	2
Lowest 20%	5	7
Lowest 40%	14	18
Highest 40%	72	65
Highest 20%	51	41
Highest 5%	26	14

Total population

Percent earned by	Total	Excluding expatriates
Lowest 5%	3	4
Lowest 20%	15	16
Lowest 40%	30	32
Highest 40%	52	50
Highest 20%	33	30
Highest 5%	16	11

Source: Mission calculations based on the 1970 Census of Agriculture Report, and the 1972/73 Urban Household Budget Survey Report.

F. External Trade

Comprehensive balance-of-payments statistics are not available. Only statistics for exports and imports of goods have been compiled, but the published statistics are far from complete. Collection of trade statistics has been difficult, since until recently Lesotho did not maintain customs posts along its borders. Only in 1970 did the government start establishing a number of customs posts, as more accurate import figures are now needed to compute Lesotho's share in the customs and excise revenue of the customs area. Import figures up to 1970 and export figures up to now are based on questionnaires sent to traders. All figures are likely to be considerably underestimated. No comprehensive information is available on payments for and receipts from services, nor on private capital flows. By the nature of the monetary arrangements within the customs area, Lesotho cannot have either a surplus or deficit on its overall balance of payments. Unless it is offset by special balance-of-payments assistance, any external disequilibrium is absorbed through monetary contraction or expansion. The available foreign trade data provide the picture for recent years (see Table 3.6).

Table 3.6: ESTIMATED VALUE OF IMPORTS AND EXPORTS OF GOODS, 1966-1972
(In million rand)

	1966	1967	1968	1969	1970	1971	1972
Imports							
Foodstuffs, beverages, tobacco	7.1	5.4	5.5	6.7	7.2	6.9	11.7
Crude materials	0.4	0.4	0.4	0.3	0.3	0.6	0.5
Mineral fuels, etc.	1.0	1.6	1.2	1.4	1.5	1.7	2.4
Animal and vegetable oils	0.2	0.2	0.1	0.1	0.2	0.3	0.4
Chemicals	1.3	1.7	1.7	1.5	1.3	1.8	2.2
Manufactured goods	9.8	10.7	11.3	9.9	8.8	11.9	20.7
Machinery and transport equipment	2.0	2.5	2.6	2.8	3.1	4.1	5.0
Other imports	1.2	1.2	1.2	1.1	0.6	0.7	-
Total	22.9	23.8	23.9	23.9	22.9	28.0	43.0
Exports							
Live animals	0.5	1.2	1.2	0.6	0.8	0.7	0.9
Foodstuffs	0.2	0.5	0.4	0.7	1.1	0.3	0.7
Wool	a/	1.5	1.5	1.4	0.9	0.8	2.0
Mohair	a/	0.5	0.6	0.7	0.6	0.5	1.1
Diamonds	0.7	1.0	0.4	1.2	0.7	0.2	0.2
Other exports	0.2	0.2	0.1	0.2	0.2	0.4	1.1
Total	a/	4.9	4.2	4.9	4.2	3.0	6.1
Trade deficit	a/	18.9	19.7	19.0	18.7	25.0	36.9

a/ No comparable figures available.

Source: Appendix Table 3.1.

The import figures through 1970, assuming that they are collected on a year-by-year comparable basis, corroborate the picture of a stagnant economy. The sharp increase after 1970 reflects a better collection of data. The possibilities for improving the coverage even more do not seem to be exhausted yet. The government is very diligent in this matter, so that for a few more years to come increases in recorded imports can be expected. The recorded exports are very low. Recorded exports from the livestock sector (live animals, wool, and mohair) were on the average about R2 million a year over the last six years. With a national herd comprising about 0.5 million cattle, 1.5 million sheep, and one million angora goats, it is almost inconceivable that actual exports from the livestock sector would not have been much higher. It is impossible to reconcile the apparent trade deficit of almost R40 million in 1972 with known and estimated inflows of remittances, transfers, and capital. Whatever is known of these flows (see page 17) suggests that actual exports must have been at least three times as much as recorded exports. This hypothesis is corroborated by preliminary findings of the 1973 rural income survey. All this seriously questions the vaildity of the 1966/67-1970/71 national accounts estimates recently made in the Bureau of Statistics in which the recorded import and export figures were used. Since these figures are obviously much too low, the levels of both gross domestic product and private consumption may well be higher than the estimates given in Table 3.2.

IV. GOVERNMENT OPERATIONS

A. Overall Budgetary Position and Financing

At independence the government inherited from the British administration a situation in which current expenditures were more than twice as high as current revenue. Until the end of the 1950s, the current budget was more or less in balance: expenditures were tailored to domestic revenue at a very low level of about R3 million a year. In order to prepare the country for independence (by building up a local administration and improving government services), the British administration started around 1960 to increase current expenditures. Because of Lesotho's poverty the scope for fiscal measures was limited, so the British government agreed to provide annual grants-in-aid to support the budget. After independence the British government continued to support the budget. Up to the 1968/69 period, grants-in-aid financed about half of Lesotho's current budget. Since the 1969/70 period Lesotho has received greatly increased revenue from the new customs agreement. The recurrent budget deficits decreased from about R6 million to less than R2 million in the 1972/73 period, and in the 1973/74 period a surplus of R4 million was attained. The British government decreased its grants-in-aid correspondingly and stopped them altogether in the 1973/74 period.

Before and after independence the larger part of the government's capital budget was also financed by British grants. Other external sources included a US$4.1 million IDA credit in 1966 for roads, from which disbursements were made during the 1966/67-1969/70 period, and various small grants from public and private aid organizations. In 1973 Lesotho received a US$5.6 million IDA credit and a US$2.8 million grant from USAID for the Thaba Bosiu Rural Development Project (see pages 43-44). Recently, domestic financial institutions -- such as the Post Office Savings Bank, the Lesotho Bank, and the commercial banks -- have on a small scale started contributing to government financing. Table 4.1 gives a summary of the government's budgetary position from the 1966/67 to the 1973/74 periods.

B. Recurrent Revenue

Table 4.2 illustrates the recent development and the structure of government recurrent revenue. The large increase in customs and excise receipts after the new customs agreement became operative in 1969 is very striking. Lesotho's share for the 1969/70 period and the 1970/71 period was provisionally determined on the basis of Lesotho's estimated imports (R25 million) in 1968. Because of better coverage the figure of recorded imports has increased substantially. In the 1971/72 period imports were estimated at R42 million and in the 1972/73 period at R52 million. The high figure for customs receipts in the 1973/74 period (R14.6 million) reflects not only the sharp increase in recorded imports but also an adjustment for an agreed amount of under-recording of imports in earlier years. Lesotho's customs and excise revenue for the 1974/75 period was determined at R17 million, including another readjustment for previous under-recording.

Table 4.1: CENTRAL GOVERNMENT BUDGETARY POSITION, 1966/67-1973/74
(In million rand)

	Average 1966/67-1968/69	1969/70	1970/71	1971/72	Preliminary 1972/73	Mission estimate 1973/74
Current revenue	5.2	9.0	9.1	11.1	12.0	20.6
Current expenditure	11.3	11.4	11.9	12.4	13.8	16.5
Current deficit/surplus	- 6.1	- 2.4	- 2.8	- 1.3	- 1.8	+ 4.1
Capital expenditure	3.0	1.8	2.1	3.8	3.1	5.0
Financing deficit/surplus	- 9.1	- 4.2	- 4.9	- 5.1	- 4.9	- 0.9
Financed by						
Grants						
U.K. grants-in-aid	5.2	1.6	2.0	0.9	0.6	-
U.K. capital grants a/	2.4	1.0	2.0	3.2	2.0	3.7
Other	0.4	0.5	0.5	0.4	0.1	1.0
Foreign loans						
IDA	0.9	0.1	-	-	-	0.5
UNDP	-	-	-	-	-	0.3
Domestic borrowing	0.1	0.1	0.6	0.3	0.4	0.2
Change in cash position	- 0.1	- 0.9	+ 0.2	- 0.3	- 1.8	+ 4.8

a/ Including those from private sources.

Source: Treasury annual reports and information provided by the Ministry of Finance.

In spite of the stagnant economy, local revenue has increased from some R3 million in the 1966/67 period to R6 million in the 1973/74 period. This is largely due to improved tax collection. Apart from the introduction in the 1969/70 period of a development levy payable by income tax payers and a small increase in personal income taxes, tax rates have not been increased since independence. The government feels that, in general, tax rates in Lesotho should not move out of line with those in South Africa. Personal income tax rates are somewhat higher in Lesotho than in South Africa; but company tax -- 37.5 percent of net income -- is at present substantially lower than in South Africa, where it is 45 percent. Since independence a number of foreign enterprises have established themselves in Lesotho; but, because of the tax facilities they usually enjoy, this is not yet reflected in higher company tax receipts. The basic tax is an annual tax of R3.50 payable by every male citizen above the age of 18, except when he is a student or otherwise dependent on his parents. The earnings of ministries and departments represent, for a large part, revenue from public utilities and post and telecommunication services, which are channeled through the budget, as are the expenditures on these services.

Table 4.2: CENTRAL GOVERNMENT CURRENT DOMESTIC REVENUE, 1966/67-1973/74
(In million rand)

	Average 1966/67-1968/69	1969/70	1970/71	1971/72	Preliminary 1972/73	Mission estimate 1973/74
Direct taxes	1.3	1.7	1.9	2.4	2.6	2.8
of which						
Basic tax	0.9	0.9	1.0	1.0	1.0	1.1
Graded tax	-- a/	0.1	0.2	-- a/	-- a/	-- a/
Personal income tax) Company tax)	0.4	0.6	0.2	0.3	0.3	0.3
Development levy	-	0.1	0.2	0.2	0.3	0.3
Licenses and duties	0.4	0.5	0.4	0.5	0.4	0.5
Earnings of ministries and departments	1.0	1.0	1.1	1.4	1.4	1.6
Other local revenue	0.7	0.7	0.9	1.0	0.8	1.1
Total local revenue	3.4	4.0	4.4	5.2	5.3	6.0
Customs and excise	1.8	5.0	4.7	5.9	6.7	14.6
Total	5.2	9.0	9.1	11.1	12.0	20.6

a/ Indicates less than R50,000.

Source: Treasury annual reports and information provided by the Ministry of Finance.

C. Current Expenditures

No official functional analysis of the government's current expenditures is available, but some indication may be gathered from Table 4.3 in which the mission has grouped the various budget heads and votes into a number of expenditure categories.

Table 4.3: CENTRAL GOVERNMENT RECURRENT EXPENDITURES, 1966/67-1973/74
(In million rand)

	Average 1966/67-1968/69	1969/70	1970/71	1971/72	Preliminary 1972/73	Mission estimate 1973/74
Economic services	2.5	2.3	2.6	3.0	3.3	4.1
Agriculture	0.9	1.0	1.1	1.2	1.3	
Public works	1.0	0.8	1.0	1.1	1.4	
Post and telecommunications	0.5	0.4	0.4	0.5	0.5	
Other a/	0.1	0.1	0.1	0.1	0.1	
Social services	3.2	3.2	3.0	3.3	4.0	5.0
Education	2.1	2.2	2.1	2.2	2.8	
Health	1.1	1.0	0.9	1.0	1.2	
Internal security	1.3	1.6	1.9	1.9	1.8	2.3
Police	1.0	1.3	1.6	1.5	1.5	
Prisons	0.3	0.3	0.4	0.4	0.3	
General administration	3.1	3.0	3.1	3.4	3.9	4.6
Financial obligations	1.2	1.2	1.3	0.9	0.8	0.9
Public debt service	0.2	0.2	0.2	0.2	0.3	0.3
Other b/	1.0	1.0	1.1	0.7	0.5	0.6
Total	11.3	11.4	11.9	12.4	13.8	16.5

a/ Commerce, industry, mining, tourism, and Maseru Town.
b/ Mostly pension obligations to former British officials.

Source: Treasury annual report and information provided by the Ministry of Finance.

Expenditures for the largest productive sector, agriculture, have been less than 10 percent of total expenditures; and expenditures for commerce, industry, mining, and tourism combined have averaged less than one percent of total expenditures. The expenditures for education (20 percent of the total) consist, for a large part, of subsidies to religious missions who primarily run the country's educational system. Service payments on public debt are very low and take up less than 2 percent of the recurrent budget.

One of the objectives of the First Five-Year Development Plan was to end the dependence of the recurrent budget on British grants-in-aid. Since independence, therefore, it has been a deliberate policy to restrain expenditures. Given some price increases which must have occurred, it is almost certain that expenditures in real terms declined up to the 1971/72 period. In spite of the substantially improved revenue position, the Ministry of Finance attempted to continue its severe restrictive policies in the 1973/74 period. The original budget estimate for the 1973/74 period provided for the same level as the previous year's actuals. In the course of the year, however, budgetary control was somewhat relaxed. As a result of this and of the high rate of inflation (13 percent) imported from South Africa, recurrent expenditures amounted to about R16.5 million in the 1973/74 period, R2.7 million more than in the 1972/73 period.

The policy of containing recurrent expenditures has contributed greatly to the early attainment of independence from British budget support. But this has been achieved at a price. Total recurrent expenditures in Lesotho were so low that they provided only for a bare minimum of government services. Although development-related recurrent expenditures have generally been made available if and when development projects came along, the low level of recurrent expenditures has certainly prevented the buildup of an adequate framework for planning and project preparation and implementation and is, therefore, one of the reasons why capital expenditure has remained so low (see page 32). In fact, little investigation has so far been carried out to establish, first, the likely effect on recurrent expenditures of preparing and implementing development projects; and, second, the size of long-term recurrent commitments connected with development projects. This exercise should be given high priority, as it is critical for the government in determining its own financial resources available to fund its future development program.

D. Outlook for the Recurrent Budget

It appears likely that, in future, recurrent revenue will be much higher than what, until very recently, was thought to be possible (Table 4.4). In absolute terms, the largest contribution is expected to come from customs revenue and revenue from a new diamond mine to be opened up soon (see page 47). Customs revenue for the 1974/75 period has already been fixed at R17 million, but this amount includes an element of readjustment to compensate for under-recording of imports in earlier years. Assuming that no such adjustment will be made for the 1975/76 period, customs revenue in that year will then drop to some R14.5 million. Thereafter, however, customs revenue

Table 4.4: PROJECTION OF THE GOVERNMENT RECURRENT BUDGET, 1973/74-1980/81
(In million rand)

	73/74	74/75	75/76	76/77	77/78	78/79	79/80	80/81
Direct taxes	2.8	3.6	4.5	5.2	5.9	6.6	7.3	8.0
of which								
Basic tax	1.1	1.4	1.7	1.8	1.9	2.0	2.1	2.2
Company tax	0.3	0.4	0.6	0.8	1.1	1.2	1.4	1.6
Casino	-	0.3	0.5	0.7	0.9	1.1	1.3	1.5
Other	1.4	1.5	1.7	1.9	2.0	2.3	2.5	2.7
Revenue diamond mine	-	-	2.2	5.0	5.3	5.7	6.2	6.8
Other taxes and non-tax revenue	3.2	3.4	3.8	4.2	4.6	5.1	5.6	6.1
Customs and excise	14.6	17.0	14.5	17.5	22.3	22.4	21.8	23.9
Total revenue	20.6	24.0	25.0	31.9	38.1	39.8	40.9	44.8
Recurrent expenditures	16.5	19.2	22.5	25.8	29.2	33.4	38.0	43.3
Budget surplus	4.1	4.8	2.5	6.1	8.9	6.4	2.9	1.5

Source: Mission estimates.

will increase again in step with the increase in imports. Rather conservatively, the mission assumes an average increase in normal imports of 11 to 12 percent a year -- 8 percent in price and 3 percent in real terms. In addition, the mission assumes an extra amount of imports related to the establishment of the diamond mine, totaling some R20 million during the 1974/75-1976/77 period. The diamond mine itself would yield between R5 million and R6 million a year in government revenue from the 1975/76 period onward (see page 46). The above estimate for customs revenue is a minimum in that it does not take into account that in the foreseeable future more large capital projects might be started, such as the Malibamatso water export scheme (see page 48) and a few large-scale industries. If any of these projects materialize, imports -- and hence customs revenue -- will be substantially higher than projected.

Other revenue is also expected to continue to increase. The government has announced that in the 1974/75 period the basic tax rate will be increased from R3.50 to R6.00 per head. This should yield an additional annual revenue of R0.6 million. The casino tax is payable with a lag of three years, and a first payment of R0.3 million over the 1971/72 period will be received in the 1974/75 period. Given the sharp increase in number of tourists in recent years, government income from the casino should also increase sharply. Company tax is also likely to show a substantial increase, as the tax advantages granted to several smaller industries and the Holiday Inn complex will gradually come to an end. For all other taxes and nontax revenue, the mission has assumed the same growth rates as observed over the past six years. Total local revenue may then increase from R6 million in the 1973/74 period to some R17 million by the 1980/81 period.

The expected sharp increase in revenue will allow a substantially higher level of recurrent expenditure. The First Five-Year Development Plan states as an important aim of financial policy that the government intends "to readjust the pattern of recurrent expenditure so as to increase the relative importance of the more developmental activities of government, and per contra to reduce the relative importance of administrative overheads in total expenditure." The mission is in full agreement with this objective. In spite of the improved revenue situation, the government should continue to keep increases in nondevelopment-related expenditures to a minimum. On the other hand, embarking on a more ambitious development program will undoubtedly necessitate a strong increase in development-related recurrent expenditures. To make sure, however, that most of the increase in revenue is used for developmental purposes, the budget office in the Ministry of Finance needs to be strengthened considerably; and budget control needs to be tightened. An exact estimate of the required increase is difficult to make. For projection purposes, the mission assumes that the government will allow a controlled increase in total recurrent expenditures of some 15 percent a year over the next seven years or so. Assuming a rate of inflation of 7 percent, this would mean a real growth of 8 percent a year.

Under the above assumptions with respect to revenue and expenditure, budget surpluses will be generated which should be used to finance the capital budget. The surpluses could add up to about R30 million over the next six years or so (Table 4.4). The government intends to set aside R3 million as a cushion against possible fluctuations in customs receipts in the future.

A substantial amount may be needed to alleviate the lot of returning mine workers (see page 38). Nevertheless, it would appear that all in all budget surpluses could contribute some R20 million, or R4 million a year, to the financing of the Second Plan.

E. Capital Expenditure and Absorptive Capacity

Table 4.5, which gives the government's capital expenditure from the 1966/67-1972/73 periods, is indicative of the very low level of development effort in the past and of the slow start of the First Five-Year Development Plan. The only substantial capital item completed in that period was the IDA-financed road (R2.9 million), which was constructed between 1966 and 1969. Over the period as a whole, total government capital expenditure has not been more than R3 per capita a year.

Table 4.5: CENTRAL GOVERNMENT CAPITAL EXPENDITURE, 1966/67-1972/73
(In million rand)

	Average 1966/67-1968/69	1969/70	1970/71	1971/72	Preliminary 1972/73
Productive activities	0.61	0.66	0.69	1.19	0.45
Agriculture	0.57	0.60	0.64	1.02	0.43
Mining, commerce, industry	0.04	0.06	0.05	0.17	0.02
Infrastructure	1.80	0.73	0.77	0.99	1.51
Roads	1.33	0.37	0.35	0.53	0.79
Public utilities)	0.47	0.25	0.25	0.33	0.44
Other)		0.11	0.17	0.13	0.27
Social services	0.24	0.21	0.27	0.40	0.31
Education	0.12	0.13	0.20	0.25	0.24
Health	0.12	0.08	0.07	0.15	0.07
General government services	0.35	0.17	0.41	1.25	0.87
Civil servants' housing	-	-	-	0.30	0.17
Other	0.35	0.17	0.41	0.95	0.70
Total	3.00	1.77	2.14	3.83	3.14

Source: Treasury annual reports and information from the Ministry of Finance.

In the first three years of the First Plan (1970/71-1972/73), total government capital expenditures amounted to only 56 percent of the planned target for that period (Table 4.6). Moreover, relatively more of what was intended was spent on less productive government services and relatively less on productive sectors. The pattern of actual expenditures gives a distorted picture of development priorities, which is worrying to the authorities in Lesotho. One reason for this distortion is that projects in the government sector (office buildings and so forth) are easier to prepare and implement than those in other sectors. The British policy of canceling the unused portion of capital aid commitments in any one year may also have played a role here. The government cited examples of projects of relatively low priority but easy to prepare that have been pushed forward simply to use up funds. This would have been at the expense of more productive projects which are more difficult and time consuming to prepare. These factors, however, cannot wholly explain why capital expenditures in the economic and social sectors have lagged so much behind plan targets. In the next few paragraphs, the mission will attempt to analyze the reasons for the delays, identify the general constraints to development, 1/ and discuss the measures the government is taking to make the Second Plan more successful than the First.

It would be incorrect to state that the First Plan, which called for government capital expenditures to the amount of R5.5 million to R6 million a year, was too ambitious in the sense that finance would not have been available. Although no budgetary savings were anticipated over the Plan period, there are strong indications that foreign donors among them would have been willing to provide the necessary capital assistance, had there been a choice of projects ready for implementation. Nevertheless, financial constraints have played a role in that the government's constant worries about the availability of local funds for development projects and for development-related recurrent expenditures, as well as for the total dependence on foreign capital aid, have clearly frustrated project planning and implementation.

In the future the substantially improved budgetary situation will give government much more leeway in planning. The Second Plan should be more ambitious than the First Plan in that sectoral programs and projects should be planned in the country's best development interest, irrespective of whether foreign aid has already been committed or not. Donor countries should be presented a comprehensive and practical plan, and the government should be prepared to take up those high-priority projects which are less suitable for foreign financing.

Just how large can the Second Plan be from a financial point of view? As mentioned on page 32, the mission estimated that the government's own reçurrent budget surpluses could contribute about R4 million a year over the Second Plan period (1975/76-1979/80). In addition, it would appear that if sufficient, well-prepared projects are available, foreign donors

---

1/ Specific constraints pertaining to individual sectors will be discussed in the sector sections.

Table 4.6: FIRST FIVE-YEAR DEVELOPMENT PLAN
PLANNED AND ACTUAL CAPITAL EXPENDITURE, 1970/71-1972/73

	1970/71-1972/73 totals (Million rand) Plan	Actual	Percent plan achievement
Productive activities	4.90	2.33	48
Agriculture	3.35	2.09	62
Mining	0.41	0.01	3
Commerce, industry	1.02	0.23	22
Tourism	0.12	-	0
Infrastructure	5.67	3.27	58
Roads	2.84	1.67	59
Civil aviation	0.19	0.04	21
Water, sewerage	1.80	1.02	57
Electricity	0.21	-	0
Post, telecommunications	0.63	0.54	86
Social services	3.10	0.98	32
Education	2.59	0.69	27
Health	0.51	0.29	57
General government services	2.56	2.53	99
Civil servants' housing	0.47	0.47	100
Other	2.09	2.06	99
Total	16.23	9.11	56

Source: First Five-Year Development Plan and Treasury reports.

among them would be prepared to make at least R12 million a year in capital aid available. Assuming a continuation of the past rate of increase in capital assistance, some R4 million to R5 million a year could be made available by the United Kingdom. The International Development Association (IDA) could provide some R2 million a year, the U. S. Agency for International Development (USAID) R1 million a year, Canadian International Development Agency (CIDA) R1.5 million a year, and other donors -- such as the Scandinavian countries, the Federal Republic of Germany, and various multilateral agencies -- at least R3 million a year. Local borrowing by the government could provide another R1 million a year. In all, some R17 million a year would be available to finance the government's capital program under the Second Plan. Assuming a continued inflation of about 7 percent a year, this would mean a program of about R12 million a year in constant 1972 prices, which is twice the size of the capital program under the First Plan and almost four times as much as actual capital expenditures in the recent past.

A financial program of this size will require a thorough review of the complex of factors commonly referred to as "absorptive capacity."

In the First Plan the government recognized its low absorptive capacity. The published investment program was very much of an indicative nature. The main objective of the First Plan was to lay the foundations for future economic development by exploring the development potential in the various sectors and by building the institutions necessary for plan implementation. The time and effort needed to achieve this has been underestimated, and it is in this sense that the investment program in the First Plan has turned out to be overly ambitious. Given the state of preparation of many projects and the lack of institutions at the time the Plan was published, it was simply impossible to reach quickly the target of doubling capital expenditures.

Since the inception of the First Plan, however, substantial progress has been made, particularly in the field of identifying investment opportunities. A number of preinvestment studies have been undertaken or will soon be undertaken with the help of which it should be possible to give the Second Plan a solid foundation. Details of the various individual studies will be given in the sector sections in this report. The most important studies that have been completed or are currently under way include comprehensive transportation and tourism surveys, a telecommunications development plan, a reconnaissance study for the development of electric power, and comprehensive surveys for the exploration of mineral and water resources. In the agricultural sector the UNDP Leribe Pilot Agricultural Scheme is providing a mine of technical, economic, and sociological information which will greatly enhance the preparation of further agricultural projects. A substantive rural development project (Thaba Bosiu) has already been formulated, and implementation has already started. A study of the livestock sector is being planned. Last but not least, a comprehensive survey of the industrial sector has been carried out.

Progress with improving sector knowledge has been impressive. On the other hand, however, progress with the building of institutions for development has been less than satisfactory. It would appear that, if no firm action is taken soon, this will constitute the main constraint to achieving a considerably higher level of capital expenditures in the Second Plan period. The First Plan stressed the critical importance of creating an administrative frame for planning and plan implementation. Success with planning, however, is still too much dependent on the persuasiveness of the Planning Office and its good standing with the various ministries. Cooperation and coordination among ministries and between the ministries and the Planning Office urgently need to be institutionalized, more so as many future projects in high-priority fields -- such as rural development and education -- will cut across the responsibilities of several ministries. From an organizational point of view, it would appear desirable to merge the Planning Office and the Ministry of Finance into one ministry and to combine the present, unrelated activities of the Ministry of Finance -- such as commerce, industry, mines, and labor -- into a new ministry.

The First Plan also called for the establishment of sectoral programming units in the various executing ministries. It was a sound conception to give primary responsibility for the preparation and implementation of development projects to units in the ministries most concerned with the subject. The Planning Office would mainly have an overall coordinating and evaluation function. Apart from the Ministry of Agriculture, however, no operative sectoral programming units have been established yet. This should have very high priority. In the past the creation of new posts for this purpose was clearly hampered by budgetary constraints. In the future the financial position will be much brighter, and a substantial part of increased revenue should be set aside to increase the administrative capacity of the country. As experienced local manpower is scarce, this will require a substantially increased technical assistance input from outside. It should, however, also be possible to economize on the manpower available. The government realizes that up to now the scarce planning staff has been preoccupied with numerous very small and largely unrelated individual projects. The situation in the Ministry of Agriculture is a case in point. In the 1973/74 government capital estimates, the total cost (over a number of years) of all agricultural projects in execution or planned to start in the 1973/74 period amounts to R8 million. The four largest projects alone account for R7 million, and the remainder -- R1 million -- is divided over a variety of thirty-eight different projects of on the average less than R30,000 each. Since small projects are often not less difficult or time-consuming to prepare than large projects, the costs in terms of precious manpower are obvious. Abandoning the previous piecemeal approach to planning and concentrating instead on fewer but much larger and broadly conceived sector programs would lead to a more efficient use of manpower.

V. THE SECTORS

A. Agriculture

Characteristics of the sector

Agriculture is the largest productive sector in Lesotho; it provides an important source of income for about 85 percent of the people and contributes about 45 percent of GDP. Most of the production is for direct home consumption; only about one-third of farm output (mostly animal products) is sold. Farming is generally primitive and yields are low. Only about 13 percent of the country -- or some 900,000 acres -- is suited to crop cultivation. Most of the arable land is in the lowlands, the foothills, and the river valleys in the mountains. Maize and sorghum, grown on about 60 percent of the cultivated area, are the principal foodcrops. Wheat -- on 30 percent of the land -- is grown in the mountains as a summer crop and in the lowlands and foothills as a winter crop. Most wheat is sold in South Africa. Also, beans and peas have become increasingly valuable exports. The country is not self-sufficient in basic foodstuffs.

With some 0.5 million cattle, 1.6 million sheep, and one million goats, the country has a sizable livestock population. Most farmers who cultivate crops own a small number of livestock. Animals graze mountain pastures in summer and lowland pastures and crop residues in winter. In spite of the large numbers, the cash income derived from livestock is low. Total recorded exports from the livestock sector (live animals, wool, and mohair) were on the average no more than R2 million a year in recent years. Even if we assume that actual exports are three times as much as recorded exports, total cash income from livestock would not amount to much. The main reason for this is that many farmers, in particular those living in the lowlands and foothills, do not keep livestock for the purpose of deriving a cash income from it. Studies in connection with the Leribe Pilot Agricultural Scheme (in the lowlands) revealed that cattle are held principally for traction at ploughing time to meet social obligations and as a store of wealth and prestige. Sheep and goats are principally held for domestic slaughter, only in the second place for their wool and mohair. Small stock are also very important as everyday currency and are often used in sale or exchange for school fees, clothes, government taxes, and so forth. In the mountain region, however, livestock has a more important economic function. Farmers there own more animals, and farm income derived from livestock in the mountains is about three times as high as in the rest of the country (see pages 39-40).

Information on trends and developments in the agricultural sector is scarce. Only very recently has the Bureau of Statistics started compiling production statistics. However, agricultural censuses held in 1950, 1960, and 1970 provide a fairly reliable broad picture of overall development and characteristics of the industry. With respect to crops, the picture is most alarming (Table 5.1).

The dramatic decrease in crop yields over the two decades is very striking. The total area of arable land has remained about the same -- some

...0,000 acres; but the area of land fallow decreased from 207,000 acres in 1950 to 95,000 acres in 1970, which suggests that (because of the population pressure) land is not properly rested at present. The reasons for the sharp decline in yields of all crops are progressing soil erosion and bad husbandry practices, which have led to depletion of the soil. The 1970 census reveals that 84 percent of the farmers never use fertilizers. Manure is burnt as fuel and crop residues are used as fodder, so that no organic matter returns to the soil.

Table 5.1: PRODUCTION AND YIELDS OF MAJOR CROPS

Production (thousand metric tons)	1950	1960	1970
Maize	214	121	67
Sorghum	49	54	57
Wheat	50	58	58
Peas	8	12	5
Beans	1	1	4
Crop yields (200-pound bag per acre)			
Maize	5.3	3.7	2.3
Sorghum	4.0	3.8	3.1
Wheat	4.5	3.8	2.4
Peas	4.5	3.3	1.8
Beans	1.5	1.6	1.0

Source: Agricultural census reports.

The country is at present not in a position to feed itself properly. Recorded maize imports increased from 14,000 tons in 1960 to 45,000 tons in 1970. These figures are indicative only of the general trend in food grain imports, as imports in both years are likely to be considerably underrecorded. Lesotho exports unmilled wheat but imports wheat flour and is on the whole a net importer of wheat products. Several agencies -- such as the World Food Program, the Freedom from Hunger Campaign, and Catholic Relief Services -- provide food aid. Nevertheless, hunger and near-starvation remain common phenomena in years of drought.

The information on livestock in the agricultural censuses is thought to be less reliable than the data on crops. According to the censuses, the number of livestock has generally increased over the years; but the figures of recorded exports suggest that the cash output from livestock has not kept pace with the increase in animals (Table 5.2).

Under present husbandry practices, the number of livestock exceeds the carrying capacity of the land. Lack of grazing control has led to a serious deterioration of mountain pastures. Together with uncontrolled breeding, this has affected the quality and productivity of the animals. Not only has output stagnated, but there is now a severe shortage of sufficiently strong draft animals at ploughing time. The worsening ecological situation in the mountains has led to a movement of people and animals to the lowlands

Table 5.2: NUMBER OF LIVESTOCK AND EXPORTS OF LIVESTOCK PRODUCTS

Livestock (thousand head)	1950	1960	1970	
Cattle	431	546	552	
Sheep	1,577	1,466	1,655	
Goats	609	671	973	
Exports	**Average 1949-51**	**Average 1959-61**	**Average 1969-71**	**1972**
Cattle (thousand head)	10.6	10.2	11.8	8.9
Wool (million pounds)	12.1	7.1	9.2	7.9
Mohair (million pounds)	1.6	1.5	2.2	1.8

Source: Agricultural census reports and annual bulletins of statistics.

and foothills, adding to the pressure on the land there. In 1960 almost 30 percent of the rural population lived in mountain areas, while in 1970 only 20 percent lived there. Also, in absolute numbers the population of the mountain areas has decreased.

Current grazing practices have also a harmful socioeconomic side effect. The absence of fencing makes it necessary that herds are accompanied by people in order to keep livestock from straying into cropland and to prevent theft. Most of the herding is done by boys who should be attending school. The number of herdboys is estimated at between 60,000 and 70,000. This is corroborated by school enrollment figures. Many more girls enroll in school than boys: in 1970, 72,000 boys were enrolled in primary schools as against 104,000 girls. Also, the dropout rate for boys is reported to be higher than for girls.

The 1970 Agricultural Census provides valuable information on the characteristics of the farming household, which is the basic decision-making unit of production. There are about 187,500 farm households in Lesotho. Of those, some 185,000 have land for crop cultivation. The majority of the landless farm households owns some livestock which is grazed on communal land. The typical farm household with land consists of five to six family members. Adult males of working age are often working in South Africa. In 1970 on 51 percent of the farms, there was no male head of the household present.

The characteristics of the farmholdings vary by region. The 1970 census report gives a breakdown by four regions: the lowlands, the foothills, the mountains, and the Orange River Valley. Although farmers in the foothills and the Orange River Valley are generally poorer than those in the lowlands, the characterisitics of farm households in these three regions are much the same. The assets of the average farm holding there are 5 to 5.5 acres of arable land, three heads of cattle, and ten to twelve sheep and goats. In the mountains farm households have less arable land (4 acres on the average) but own more livestock: on the average four heads of cattle and more than thirty sheep and goats. Farmers in the mountains seem to be more commercially oriented than farmers elsewhere in Lesotho. At the 1970 census 8.5 percent of the

Table 5.3: ESTIMATED INCOME OF RURAL HOUSEHOLDS, 1970

	Lowlands	Foothills	Mountains	Orange River Valley	Total Lesotho
Number of households	72,080	57,740	39,590	18,020	187,430
Number of persons	388,670	291,030	211,480	96,770	987,950
Estimated annual income per household (Rand) of which:					
from crop cultivation	53.35	41.35	40.75	31.80	45.75
from livestock 1/	30.70	26.45	81.45	37.15	40.75
total farm income	84.05	67.80	122.20	68.95	86.50
from labor in South Africa	93.80	78.00	57.80	92.50	81.20
from labor in Lesotho	21.50	15.45	17.55	24.25	19.05
total income	199.35	161.25	197.55	188.70	186.75

1/ Includes cattle, sheep, goats, pigs, and poultry.

Source: Mission estimates based on the 1970 Census of Agriculture Report.

farmers in the mountains reported to produce mainly for sale. In the rest of the country, the percentage was only 2.5. Also the take-off rate of cattle is higher in the mountains (7.5 percent) than elsewhere in Lesotho (5.5 percent). Because of this, farm incomes in the mountains are higher than in the other parts of Lesotho. In the lowlands, the foothills, and the Orange River Valley, however, a larger portion of the people seek to supplement farm incomes by working in South Africa, so that the inequalities in total household income by region are much less than those in farm income only (Table 5.3).

The main constraints to development of the small farming units have been lack of knowledge of modern farming practices; lack of credit and marketing facilities; and a shortage of male labor, as well as of draft animals at the time of field preparation and planting. According to the 1970 Agricultural Census, 50 percent of the heads of farm households are illiterate; and 75 percent have had less than a full primary school education. Government and a number of private and official organizations have attempted over a long period of time to encourage the formation of cooperatives and credit societies; but in 1970, 94 percent of the farm households were not members of any marketing society, tractor cooperative, or credit society. In 1970 less than 35 percent of the farm households owned draft animals or tractors. The others had to borrow or hire means of traction with the result that their fields were often not ready at the proper time of planting.

The shortage of male labor and traction as well as the lack of credit facilities have led to a spontaneous growth of the institution of sharecropping. The extent of sharecropping is not precisely known, and also the economics of sharecropping have not been sufficiently investigated. It is thought, however, that at present some 25 percent of the land is cultivated under various sharecropping arrangements. In sharecropping, the landholder engages in a deal with a sharecropper (who could be another farmer or, more frequently, a contractor) whereby the latter provides traction, implements, seeds, and labor in return for a part of the harvest. The sharecropper usually has better access to commercial credit than the individual farm household. The deals are normally one of two types. The traditional and most common type is that the contractor takes care of ploughing and planting. At harvest time he gets 50 percent of all produce after deduction of his cash inputs for seed and fertilizer. Under the second type of deal, which has emerged more recently as a result of labor shortage, the contractor handles everything from ploughing to transport of the harvest and takes two-thirds of all produce for his effort. Another, less common type of sharecropping is field sharing, by which contractors or members of landless families work on all the land of a farm household and keep the harvest from one of the landholder's two or three fields.

It is sometimes believed in Lesotho that sharecropping is exploitative in the economic sense in that it encourages the rise of a class of agricultural capitalists and economic domination of the many by the few. Nevertheless, there are indications that sharecroppers are taking the greater risk at present; and, in any case, they are performing a useful role in a situation in which male labor and draft animals are scarce. Without their services much land would remain fallow, and many fields would be prepared at the wrong time.

Government policies and programs

At the time of the inception of the First Five-Year Development Plan of 1970/71-1974/75, government recurrent expenditure for agriculture ran at about R1 million a year; capital expenditure at about R0.6 a year. These low levels are indicative of the lack of development effort in the past. What capital expenditure there was, was mainly confined to some improvements of existing facilities and to some small pilot developments in conservation and irrigation. The main effort of the Ministry of Agriculture was in the lowlands and was aimed at slowing down the alarming rate of erosion. Unfortunately, soil conservation was not tied in with agricultural development programs. As no other services were offered to the farmer, conservation works were soon neglected and erosion continued.

In the First Plan the highest priority is attached to increasing agricultural productivity in both the crop and livestock sectors through the strengthening and expansion of existing services to the farmer. The long-term development objective for crop production is to transform crop farming from its present subsistence basis to the production of cash crops for import substitution and export. Increased crop production is to be attained by introducing better husbandry methods which would give an increase in crop yields and would make possible a shift in production towards high-value cash crops -- such as wheat, peas, and beans. The productivity of the livestock sector is to be increased mainly through training of farmers in all aspects of animal husbandry, particularly with a view to changing the traditional attitudes of the people towards livestock, and through the introduction of pasture management and grazing control.

Government capital expenditure on agriculture in the First Plan was to increase from R0.6 million a year to R1.6 million a year. In the first three years of the Plan, however, not more than about R0.7 million a year was, in fact, spent. This is mainly due to the fact that the Plan was very much of an indicative nature and that, apart from the UNDP Agricultural Pilot Scheme, it did not yet contain any substantial, well-prepared programs or projects. Experience with the UNDP pilot project, however, has been an invaluable help in preparing other agricultural schemes. A project has been prepared to expand the pilot scheme into a full-fledged, integrated, rural development scheme (see page 43). More or less along the lines of the UNDP pilot scheme, another substantial rural development project (the Thaba Bosiu project, see below) was prepared with the help of the Bank and USAID, implementation of which started in 1973. As a follow-up to the pilot scheme, UNDP started in 1972 an agricultural extension project in the poorest part of the country, the Orange River Valley (the Senqu Scheme). All these projects concentrate on dryland farming and are easily replicable. Continuing these efforts, it should be possible to increase capital expenditure on agriculture much above the R1.6 million-a-year level envisaged in the First Plan.

In the First Plan the government envisaged that nearly half of the capital expenditure for crop production was to go for irrigation. This emphasis on irrigation developed when a series of droughts had seriously affected agricultural production in Lesotho. A considerable amount of study, however, is needed to establish clearly the economics of irrigation. Only a few small irrigation projects, totaling some 700 acres, have been undertaken with the assistance of bilateral donors. Not much is known about the results, but they are thought to be uneconomic. Under the program of special measures to assist the least developed countries, UNDP is planning to establish a pilot irrigation project of some 300 acres. In contrast to the Leribe Scheme, which (according to its terms of reference) had to work within existing tenure arrangements, the irrigation project would try to achieve the consolidation of individual holdings into a single production unit, which appears to be essential for carrying out irrigation projects of any substantial size. The country's irrigation potential is not precisely known. Tentatively, a total area of some 41,000 acres of irrigable land has been identified, which is less than 5 percent of all arable land. The capital costs and overheads to develop irrigable land will be very high; and, in any case, it will affect only small portions of the population.

The UNDP Pilot Agricultural Scheme (total cost R1.5 million), which started operations in 1970, is the first substantial agricultural development scheme undertaken in Lesotho. It covers an area of 5,000 acres of arable land near Leribe. The scheme is designed to demonstrate the impact on production and income of an integrated approach to agricultural development within the existing framework of land tenure. It concentrates on the application of relatively simple package of inputs, including mechanization, improved seed, insecticides, fertilizer, and extension services. It includes also a substantial element of training of agricultural staff as well as soil conservation works.

In the three years that the project has been operating, it has been demonstrated that farmers are responsive to improved agricultural techniques. Yields of traditional crops doubled and so did cash incomes. A beginning was also made with the introduction of new, higher-value crops, such as sunflower seed and potatoes. An interesting feature is also that a system of hail insurance was introduced which met with great success and which the government intends to introduce countrywide. The increase in cash incomes to the farmers from less than R20 a year to some R40 a year is encouraging; but, because of alternative employment opportunities in South Africa where unskilled workers earn up to R300 a year, there is no evidence yet that men have preferred to stay on their farms because of the project. The scarcity of adult male labor has led the project management to concentrate on contractors who are involved in sharecropping. It has established a core of supervised contractors who are taught dryland farming and soil conservation techniques as well as in bookkeeping.

The UNDP scheme will gradually be phased out by 1975 and will then be incorporated into a much larger agricultural project in the adjacent Khomokhoana catchment area. The Khomokhoana project, which comprises some 32,000 acres of arable land, may cost up to R3 million. The project will be implemented by FAO with Swedish financial assistance.

In the meantime an even larger dryland farming project was prepared with assistance from the Bank and USAID, the implementation of which started in 1973. The Thaba Bosiu Rural Development Project is situated in the Little Caledon catchment area. As designed, the project comprised: the timely provision to about 12,000 peasant farmers of improved seed, fertilizer, and cultivation services; the credit to acquire them; technical agricultural guidance in their use; marketing of the crop; road development; and soil conservation. Over six years, including about one year of planning and preparation, it would improve maize, sorghum, wheat, and bean production on about 60,000 acres of land and extend dairy farming through the supply of 400 good-grade cows to selected farms. Integrated farming would be gradually introduced, including improved production of livestock. During the first year of planning and preparation, it was found feasible to broaden the scope of the project. Horticulture will be introduced, and more attention than originally intended will be given to livestock. The project is administered by an autonomous project authority within the government. The total cost of the project is estimated at R7.75 million (US$12 million), to which IDA contributes US$5.6 million and USAID US$2.8 million. USAID is mainly concerned with the soil conservation component of the project.

The project would work with and provide credit to farm associations, and it would provide tractors to experienced contractors. In contrast to the UNDP pilot scheme where the supervised contractors continued their operations on the basis of sharecropping, tractor operators will be required to offer their services for cash, which it is hoped will prevent exploitation of the farmer by the contractor. The benefits to the farmers in the project area are estimated as follows. In place of subsistence with an annual cash income of R18 to R20, a wheat farmer would have, in addition to his subsistence, about R55 annual net cash income, a maize and sorghum farmer about R45. Both would have the prospect of integrated farming with net income, from the same acreage, well above R100. One milk cow would produce an annual net income of about R50.

Another project in the south of Lesotho, the UNDP Sengu River Agricultural Extension Project, is in its preparatory year of operations. At a cost of $1.4 million, the project will make a start with agricultural development in the southern lowlands through strengthening the extension services in two districts. Extension efforts will concentrate on livestock production, run-of-the-river irrigation, consolidated dryland farming, range management, and conservation. Efforts will also be made to encourage farmers to block their land.

All four projects mentioned above have in common that they basically concentrate on crop cultivation and attempt to improve livestock production on the fringe. The government is strongly of the opinion that the cattle industry has a major potential for development. The national herd exceeds half a million head, while the recorded annual revenue from sales is less than R1 million. Because of the temperate climate and high altitude, the country is remarkably free from animal diseases. Officials in the Ministry of Agriculture think that the traditional attitudes towards cattle are not as great an obstacle to progress as is commonly thought. What is lacking is a comprehensive plan for livestock development. The government plans to draw up a program and has requested CIDA, the World Bank, and USAID to provide a team to assist in the identification and formulation of a major livestock project. There are two other developments in the livestock sector to to be noted. First, the Danish International Development Agency (DANIDA) has been requested to assist in the establishment of an export abattoir. Second, legislation was passed in December 1973 for the establishment of a livestock marketing cooperation.

Constraints on development

As in most developing countries, the major constraints on improving agricultural production are tenurial and institutional. Experience with the Leribe Pilot Agricultural Scheme and, so far, with the Thaba Bosiu Rural Development Project has not borne out views previously held that the land tenure is a major constraint on the improvement of crop cultivation. Much more needed than tenurial changes is better land-use planning within the existing tenurial system. By contrast, the future development of the livestock industry in the mountain areas is wholly dependent on tenurial changes. Under the existing system it is impossible to exert control over grazing, breeding, and stock numbers; and the result is an increase in numbers of livestock, overgrazing, and uncontrolled breeding with a consequent detrimental effect on the natural pastures and the quality of livestock. Speedy enactment and enforcement of the drafted regulations which will make fencing of mountain pastures and rotational grazing possible (see page 11) are absolutely essential to future livestock development.

Government institutions and services

It is the government's intention to strengthen and expand its services to the farmer, although it realizes that Lesotho, being a small country with limited resources, cannot afford to have over-elaborate organizations. The present institutions and services in the agricultural sector, however, are far from adequate and are a serious constraint to future development.

In recent years the planning unit in the Ministry of Agriculture has been strengthened considerably, which has led to the preparation of the various substantial projects discussed above. However, the Ministry is still particularly weak on the implementation side. Most of the large projects under way are executed through separate project authorities, staffed by expatriates. This may have been the only way to achieve quick results, but there is a built-in tendency for the project to be managed independently of existing government departments and institutions and in isolation of overall sector programs. Moreover, the projects in execution have seriously depleted the Ministry's own staff. If the present projects are to be repeated or followed up, a considerable further strengthening of the Ministry's staff is necessary.

Of particular concern is the severe shortage of supporting staff at lower levels, particularly of extension workers. This shortage is already felt in the execution of the present projects. The output of the Lesotho Agricultural College is not sufficient, and the college is not being run satisfactorily at present. However, assistance has been requested from the British government, which has offered both capital to expand and improve the facilities at the college as well as technical assistance to strengthen the teaching staff. If this goes ahead soon, the supply of suitably trained agricultural staff is likely to improve considerably after 1977.

There is a conspicuous lack of credit for the purchase of farm inputs. About 130 thrift and credit societies have been registered as cooperatives in Lesotho. Other sources of agricultural credit include the Agricultural Development Fund (ADF), which is administered directly by the Ministry of Agriculture; Co-op Lesotho; and the Lesotho Credit Union Scheme for Agriculture (LECUSA). ADF's function is to channel funds obtained through foreign aid, especially from voluntary agencies, to farm associations. Co-op Lesotho provides credit to its member farmer cooperatives. LECUSA was established at the initiative of the Catholic Relief Service, the Oxford Relief Fund (OXFAM), and the University of Botswana, Lesotho, and Swaziland (UBLS) extension service. It provides medium-term credit to its members (seventeen at present) for the purchase of tractors and other farm equipment. Most of these credit institutions, however, have in common that they are poorly managed and that they have poor repayment records. Most of them are in financial difficulties. The extent to which credit is provided has remained very limited. In the 1970 Agricultural Census, 96 percent of the farmers reported that they had no access to any credit facilities.

The government, recognizing the need for better credit provision, established in 1972 the government-owned Lesotho Bank. The primary function of this bank was to provide credit on a nationwide scale to small Basotho businessmen as well as farmers. It was to incorporate all existing agricultural credit institutions. However, owing to a lack of cooperation from these institutions and to the fact that the attention of the management of the new Lesotho Bank has been diverted to the Lesotho National Development Corporation (see page 50), no progress has been made with establishing a suitable credit institution for agriculture. For lack of a better alternative, credit for the largest agricultural project under way (the Thaba Bosiu project) is presently being channeled through the project authority. In view of the fact that credit will play a critical role in all future major agricultural projects, this is clearly an unsatisfactory situation. Developing the Lesotho Bank into a viable credit institution for agriculture should, therefore, have very high priority.

The Basotho farmer is largely dependent on some 200 private (South African) traders for the sale of his produce. All produce from Lesotho is marketed in South Africa either for internal consumption or for reexport. Because of the various control boards in South Africa, Lesotho's commodities have the benefit of a high-priced market and are able to enjoy similar protection benefits as given to South African farmers. Thus, except for wool and mohair (the prices of which are determined in the world market), the Basotho farmer can enjoy stable and high commodity prices for the majority of his produce.

The government, however, is concerned as to whether all possible benefits are really passed on to the farmer. Because of poor infrastructure and the absence of a clear-cut government policy on marketing, the private traders have developed a quasimonopoly, leaving the farmer in a weak bargaining position. Although legislation has been passed for the establishment of a Livestock Marketing Corporation and a Produce Marketing Corporation, there is still considerable discussion as to what form national marketing institutions should take and what functions they should assume. One thought is to introduce one-channel marketing, but Lesotho is desperately short of local expertise and facilities to take over the functions of the private traders. The best solution probably would be to establish relatively small bodies with the function of introducing grading standards and exerting overall control over the private traders who should be encouraged to act as agents for the national marketing institutions.

B. Mining

Lesotho's only known mineral resource with commercial potential is diamonds. A few hundred Basotho dig for diamonds in the northern mountain region. With use of only primitive hand tools, their production is low. Moreover, output has declined in recent years because diggers were resettled from more productive sites to less productive ones to make place for exploration activities by international mining groups. The government receives 15 percent tax on the export value of diamonds.

Table 5.4: EXPORTS OF DIAMONDS, 1966-1972

Year	Weight (thousand carat)	Value (thousand rand)
Average 1966-69	19.0	816
1970	16.5	652
1971	6.8	212
1972	9.0	196

Source: Annual Report, Department of Mines, 1972.

In the last few years, a number of international mining groups prospected for diamonds in areas where local diggers had been removed. Rio Tinto prospected at Letseng-la Terai, Lonrho at Mothae, and Newmont Mining at Kao. Claiming lack of feasibility, all three mining companies decided not to embark on further investments. Subsequently, however, Anglo-De Beers took over the license from Rio Tinto at Letseng-la Terai and has decided to establish a medium-scale mine, providing employment for almost 500 people. The mine will be constructed in two years at a cost of about R20 million. The government will take a 25 percent equity participation to be paid out of future dividends. Government tax revenue in the form of sales duties and company tax will amount to about 63 percent of profits.

Over an area of 1,800 square miles outside the areas given to the mining groups for prospecting, UNDP has since 1971 been carrying out a project for diamond exploration. A number of new kimberlite pipes have been discovered, but more work is needed to determine whether they contain any diamonds in exploitable quantities. UNDP has extended its original project to do this and also to expand mineral exploitation over the rest of the country. The government has requested the Canadian government to finance an aeromagnetic survey over the southern part of Lesotho to supplement the findings of the UNDP survey.

The government is considering returning the prospecting areas abandoned by Lonrho and Newmont to local diggers. It has asked UNDP to start a pilot project for diamond exploitation under the program of special measures to assist the least developed countries. The project, which would be at the Kao site abandoned by Newmont Mining, would aim at determining whether the productivity of local diggers can be increased through improved but still labor-intensive methods.

Although the prospects for finding oil in Southern Africa do not seem bright, LNDC and the government signed an agreement in November 1972 with Westrans Petroleum Inc. of New York for the prospecting of oil. The agreement provides for LNDC to have a 30 percent equity participation in the undertaking should oil be discovered. A 5 percent royalty would have to be paid to the government, who would also receive a 50 percent profit tax.

C. Water Resources

The high mountains of Lesotho are a rich source of flowing water, but nevertheless large areas of the country suffer frequent droughts. Topographical and geographical conditions limit the opportunities for irrigation to some 41,000 acres. Water supplies for domestic use are insufficient, and the existing capacity is often stretched to its limits.

For many years plans have been investigated and discussed to use the water resources of the country for the production of hydroelectric power and for direct export of water to South Africa. Surveys in the early 1950s concentrated on the potential use of water for hydropower; but later it was thought that the best potential was for export of water by diverting the headwaters of the Malibamatso River, one of the tributaries of the Orange River, to the northern border. It is to the north of Lesotho where, in the Vaal Basin and the Witwatersrand area, most of South Africa's mining and heavy industries are located and where a shortage of water had rapidly become apparent.

In 1969 the Governing Council of UNDP approved to finance a special fund study on the water resources development in Lesotho with the Bank as executing agency. The study on water resources development was completed in 1971 by a team of consultants. The study gives basic information on supply of and needs for water in Lesotho and contains a detailed feasibility report on a water export scheme, the Malibamatso project. An important conclusion of the study is that Lesotho would not deprive itself of its own domestic water resources needed if it were to divert water to South Africa in the quantities foreseen under the Malibamatso project.

The Malibamatso project would cost about R85 million and would consist of the construction of a dam below the confluence of the Pelaneng and Malibamatso Rivers as well as a 60-kilometer tunnel northward through the Maluti mountains into the Vaal catchment area. It was intended to be constructed between 1973 and 1977 and would supply water to South Africa at a rate of 8 cubic meters per second. The Bank had agreed to finance the final design and engineering study for the project and to participate in the financing of the construction, provided that South Africa would agree to a water sales contract giving Lesotho a reasonable financial return above debt service and would provide a substantial portion of project finance.

Apart from increased government revenue from water sales, benefits to the Lesotho economy would be as follows: (a) up to 1,900 laborers would be employed during construction; (b) imports needed for the project will raise Lesotho's share of revenue under the Southern African Customs Agreement by an estimated total of R10 million; and (c) the access road to the project and the presence of a large body of water would encourage tourism development in the region.

Meetings on project conditions were held between the governments of Lesotho and South Africa in 1971 and 1972, but no agreement was reached. Discussions have since been in abeyance, and further negotiations may take place only after solutions have been found at the highest political levels for a number of problems between Lesotho and South Africa not related to the Malibamatso project itself. In the meantime, the government has requested the Swedish government to finance a study of alternative water uses, should the Malibamatso project fall through.

D. Manufacturing Industries

In pre-independence days manufacturing industries were of no practical importance in Lesotho. The 1967 Census of Production records twelve establishments (three in the public sector and most of the rest printing shops or missions) with total turnover of less than R1 million and employing just over 500 people. Accordingly, the contribution of the sector to GDP, 0.8 percent in the 1966/67 period, was very small. Since then a number of small new industries have sprung up, mainly in cooperation between foreign investors and the Lesotho National Development Corporation. The industrial sector may now contribute 2.5 to 3 percent of GDP and employ between 1,500 and 2,000 persons.

In the First National Development Plan, the government looked to the industrial sector to contribute most to reaching the target of creating 2,000 to 3,000 new jobs a year. Actual employment creation has remained far behind this target. The government's industrial policy is, first, to attract foreign investors through the promotional activities of LNDC and, second, to promote the development of indigenous small enterprises by strengthening business extension services and by establishing credit facilities. In both fields the achievements have been disappointing so far.

LNDC was established by the government as a statutory corporation in 1967. Up to 1973 it was managed by a South African businessman. LNDC has attracted investments of about R15 million, a third of which was accounted for by the Holiday Inn hotel and casino complex in Maseru and the rest by some twenty small industries on two industrial estates as well as the Lesotho Housing Corporation. These investments provided about 2,000 jobs, implying an investment cost of R7,000-R8,000 per job created.

At the end of the fiscal year ended March 31, 1973, LNDC was still very liquid. Its assets totaled R2.9 million, including only R0.4 million in shares in associated companies, R0.1 million in loans, R0.4 million in industrial estates and factory buildings, while residential land and buildings (R0.5 million) and bank deposits and other liquid funds (R1.5 million) accounted for the balance. Thus, LNDC has made only a small contribution towards the financing of the enterprises attracted. Two factors explain in part LNDC's liquidity. First, LNDC has been successful in expanding its equity, which on March 31, 1973, totaled R2.9 million; and, second, a R600,000 loan made for the Holiday Inn complex was prepaid by the borrower in 1972.

LNDC has no share capital. Its main sources of income are a commercial agreement with the Durban Sugar Exchange (which pays LNDC R400,000 a year for its sugar monopoly in Lesotho) and revenue from mining exploration rights. As this amounts to general government revenue foregone, LNDC is indirectly subsidized by the government. LNDC is also exempted from income tax. Income from investments and deposits represent less than 20 percent. During LNDC's first three years, funds were also obtained from the United Kingdom (R79,000 in expenditure grants and R105,000 in capital grants). LNDC's liabilities include loans from the Commonwealth Development Corporation (almost R200,000) and from the Lesotho Bank (R650,000). Although -- as can be seen from Appendix Table 6.3 -- LNDC would have incurred losses every year since it started operations without the income from the sugar trade monopoly and mining exploration leases, its equity has been built up and its capital structure improved.

LNDC handles for prospective investors all negotiations with the government and all matters related to company registrations, license applications, and so forth. It was also instrumental in the enactment of the Pioneer Industries Encouragement Act of 1969, which provides for generous tax incentives to foreign investors in pioneer industries. The incentives include a choice between a six-year tax holiday or depreciation allowances of up to 150 percent of the initial investment during the first year of operation, a citizen training allowance equal to 110 percent of the cost to the manufacturer, and a citizen wage allowance equal to 10 percent of the wages paid to Basotho. The incentives related to the training and employment of Basotho are particularly innovative and useful in Lesotho's context. Nevertheless, the whole package of incentives tends to change the relative prices of capital and labor in favor of capital, whereas it should be the other way around. The government is presently rethinking its incentives policy. In designing a new policy, the government might wish to consider to give much more weight to tax facilities related to the cost of training and the wage bill and less weight to depreciation allowances.

LNDC has been successful in making a beginning with industrial and tourism development in Lesotho. Although its achievements have remained much below the government's expectations, it is difficult to ascertain whether realistically much more could have been achieved. Outside South Africa Lesotho is not well known, and South African investors seem to prefer proximity to their own markets as transport costs to and from Lesotho are high. The government criticizes LNDC for not having been active enough in attracting large-scale industries to Lesotho. There is some evidence that collusion of South African interests and existing administrative and cartel arrangements in South Africa have prevented some large industries from coming to Lesotho. Another point of criticism is that, so far, LNDC has not employed any local staff. In July 1973 the contract with the South African managers of LNDC was not renewed when it expired. Since then the manager of the new Lesotho Bank has also been in charge of LNDC. Both LNDC and the Lesotho Bank are presently desperately short of staff.

Although the Lesotho Bank and LNDC have been under the same management since July 1973, it would appear advisable to keep their functions strictly separated, preferably by having a revitalized, independent LNDC. The task of promoting modern industrial development in Lesotho is very different from banking. It is basically to establish prima facie cases for investment to be followed up by feasibility studies and active promotion among prospective foreign investors, thereby advertising the advantages Lesotho has to offer, such as duty-free access to the large Southern African market and an abundant supply of workers who are already used to industrial discipline.

It is difficult to foretell how successful LNDC's new management will be. It is possible that prospective South African investors are somewhat put off by the recent changes, and it may take some time to interest industrialists from outside South Africa. However, under the provisions of the Customs Agreement, the entire Southern African market is open to industrialists in Lesotho; and LNDC should capitalize on the pressure put on industrialists in many developed countries to limit direct investment in South Africa.

At the government's request the Swedish International Development Agency (SIDA) has recently undertaken a comprehensive industrial survey with a view to establishing cases for further feasibility studies. The survey concentrated particularly on finding possibilities for the processing of Lesotho's own raw materials -- such as meat, hides, wool and mohair, grains, and building materials. At present, most raw materials for Lesotho's industries are imported from South Africa, which provides instant cash in the form of customs revenue but contributes little to the development of the rest of the economy. The SIDA report is expected to be available later in 1974.

Only very few Basotho businessmen have until now entered the field of manufacturing production, but there has been little encouragement from the government to develop local entrepreneurs except by renting out permanent workshop shells to a number of craftsmen at the Maseru market. The Business Extension Division of the Ministry of Finance, Commerce, and Industry is virtually inactive; and the new Lesotho Bank has not yet entered the field of providing credit to small local businessmen. The government recognizes the urgent need to support emerging local businessmen and is planning to establish the Basotho Enterprises Development Corporation (BEDCO), in which the functions of providing credit and extension services to small entrepreneurs would be combined. The government of Canada has been requested to provide financial and technical assistance for this undertaking.

Several attempts have been made to establish a local handicrafts industry. In 1967, following the report of an ILO expert, the government established a Village Industries Development Organization (VIDO), the function of which was to promote the production and marketing of handicraft articles. After some initial success, VIDO ran into financial difficulties, mainly because of poor management but also because of the large overheads resulting from the extension element in its activities. VIDO was liquidated in 1971, and its assets were transferred to the Lesotho Cooperative Handicrafts Society (LCH). With financial assistance from Sweden and technical assistance from ILO, LCH is stimulating production in village centers of woven mohair articles, pottery, straw hats and mats, leatherworks, semiprecious stones, and woodwork.

E. Tourism

Beautiful mountain scenery and a pleasant temperate climate are Lesotho's natural tourist attractions. Although snowfall occurs irregularly, winter sports would be possible in the highest mountains if artificial snow were used. Most of the tourists come from South Africa on short visits, particularly on weekends. The flow of tourists increased greatly after October 1970 when Amalgamated Hotels of South Africa opened a 120-room Holiday Inn with a casino at Maseru. LNDC participated in the investment of R1.6 million with a loan of R600,000, which was provided to LNDC by the Lesotho Post Office Savings Bank (now Lesotho Bank). Before the opening of the Holiday Inn complex, the number of tourists to Lesotho was on the average some 4,000 a year. However, there were an estimated 80,000 tourists in 1973. In 1972 the Holiday Inn complex was expanded with another 122 rooms and in 1973 with conference facilities for 450 persons. Total employment in tourism facilities is estimated at 600 persons, of which some 400 persons in the Holiday Inn complex alone.

Both LNDC and the Lesotho Bank are planning more investments in tourism facilities, including more hotels in Maseru and elsewhere, resort development in the mountains, and caravan and campsites along the mountain roads. Suggestions for further investment in tourism are expected to result from a comprehensive tourism survey undertaken in the 1973/74 period by Kenyan consultants under the aegis of the Commonwealth Secretariat. Their draft report is presently being considered by the government. The government's Department of Tourism (part of the Cabinet Office) is particularly weak at present and certainly not capable of carrying out or overseeing any substantial tourism development plan. The consultants envisage the formation of a Tourism Development Corporation (possibly a subsidiary of LNDC) which would promote tourism projects by direct investments in cooperation with private sector partners. Tourism development in the mountain areas will require further road development which, however, could take place in combination with road development necessary for the Malibamatso project, the diamond mine, and agricultural projects in the more remote regions of the country.

Tourism may, thus, gain in economic importance; but it will take several years before it will have become a significant industry outside the capital of Maseru. Its direct employment effect may not be very large, but substantial indirect effects would be derived in the longer run by stimulating the local production of food and handicrafts.

F. Transportation

Lesotho's basic transport system comprises about 2,000 miles of roads and tracks, a short length of railway connecting Maseru with the South African railway system, and a number of airfields and airstrips serviced by scheduled and chartered small aircraft. Because of the topography of the country, road transport is relatively easy in the north-south direction in the western lowlands but difficult in the east-west direction; therefore, air transport plays an important, if small, part in the movement of people and goods. Lack of communications between the lowlands and the rest of the country, however, still poses a problem in this small country.

Roads

The road network consists roughly of some 125 miles of tarmac roads, 500 miles of gravel roads, and almost 1,500 miles of tracks. The main road runs along the western border of the country from Butha-Buthe in the north through Maseru to Quthing in the south. Between 1967 and 1969 some 100 miles of this road -- between Leribe and Tsoaing -- were reconstructed and bituminized with the help of a US$4.1 million IDA credit. Road development after 1969 included some improvement near Maseru and Leribe, a 20-mile tarmac road branching off from the main road to Roma where the University of Botswana, Lesotho, and Swaziland (UBLS) is situated (constructed in 1972 and 1973), and a 25-mile extension of the bituminized road to Mafeting, which is presently being constructed. All later road developments have been financed by British capital grants.

Internally, Lesotho is poorly served by roads, many of which become impassable in the wet season. Formidable mountain ranges and river valleys run north and south in the central and eastern parts of the country which seriously inhibit the development of links with the east. Internal land communications with modern means of transport are, therefore, difficult. But Lesotho has some 200,000 horses and donkeys, and animal tracks play a significant role in the transportation of people and goods. Tracks are being built by local laborers under food aid programs organized by the World Food Program and the Catholic Relief Services. Standards of these tracks were very poor initially and cost of maintenance was high, but this has improved considerably with better coordination between the food aid programs and the Ministry of Works.

In the First National Development Plan, a provisional road development program for the five-year period had been drawn up; but a final choice of roads to be included in the program was to await the results of a transportation study to be carried out by the University of Stellenbosch in South Africa. This study started in 1971 but was never finished. In 1973 under the auspices of the British government (ODA), a consultant's team prepared a detailed long-term transport development plan, including road development. The Bank assisted in drawing up the terms of reference. The study has identified several investment opportunities with good economic rate of return. They comprise both roads in the lowlands and roads to open up the mountain region.

Civil aviation

Apart from the main airport -- the Leabua Jonathan Airport near Maseru -- there are thirty-one smaller airfields and airstrips in the country. Internationally, Lesotho is served by three scheduled flights a week between Maseru and Johannesburg, operated by South African Airways as well as by nonscheduled services carried out by two South African charter carriers between points in the east of Lesotho and South African towns, mainly to transport Basotho contract laborers. Most domestic services are operated by the Lesotho Airways Corporation (LAC). LAC is a state-owned company, established by the Lesotho Airways Order of 1970 in order "to provide air transport services, both scheduled and nonscheduled, domestic and international." It is a profitable company, operating a fleet of six small Cessna aircraft on five scheduled domestic lines. On a nonscheduled basis it operates flights to any of Lesotho's airfields as the need arises.

In March 1973 consultants sponsored by the Commonwealth Secretariat submitted to the government a long-term air transport development plan. The recommendations of the report include expanding internal air services by LAC; the building of some new airstrips and the improvement of facilities at existing ones; and the takeover by LAC of the scheduled services between Maseru and Johannesburg, now operated by South African Airways. Reportedly, the South African Airways' run operates at a loss; and it would be profitable to operate the line more frequently with smaller aircraft.

At present, all international air traffic to the rest of the world has to go through Johannesburg in South Africa. Leabua Jonathan Airport cannot take medium-range aircraft that would fly directly between Maseru and such places as Lusaka in Zambia and Blantyre in Malawi. In its desire to become more independent from South Africa for its international connections, the government considers building a new, larger international airport. An expert from the International Civil Aviation Organization visited Lesotho to investigate possible sites and make a prefeasibility study for such an airport. From three possible alternatives, the government selected a site at Mazenod, 10 miles from Maseru. UNDP is providing US$50,000 for a detailed feasibility study to be followed by the actual engineering and design. Preliminary estimates are that this airport would cost at least US$10 million. It would appear, however, that the expected flow of international traffic directly between Maseru and Lusaka or Blantyre is by far not large enough to justify the building of a new international airport on economic grounds alone.

G. Public Services

Electricity

Electricity is supplied by the Lesotho Electricity Corporation (LEC), a government-owned statutory corporation. Most of the electricity is bought in bulk from the Electricity Supply Commission of South Africa (ESCOM). Purchases from South Africa started in 1968 and have gradually replaced electricity generated in Lesotho. The last LEC diesel-generating station at Mohales Hoek will be shut down after completion of a transmission line from that town to Mafeteng.

Electricity consumption increased rapidly over the last years. In 1966 the Lesotho Electricity Supply Department, the forerunner of LEC, sold 4.2 million kilowatt-hours, while in the 1972/73 period LEC's sales amounted to 17 million kilowatt-hours. The connection to the South African grid has a considerable cost advantage to Lesotho; and, with increasing consumption, LEC's capital requirements have remained limited to financing substations and transmission lines. LEC is a profitable organization and raises its capital funds from commercial sources.

The government, who wishes to lessen its reliance on South Africa as the main supplier of electric energy, commissioned a reconnaissance study (sponsored by the Commonwealth Secretariat) to explore the potential for the development of hydroelectricity within Lesotho. The study identified a possible hydropower project at the Maletsunyane River near Semonkong Falls. Initial capacity of the plant, which would cost some R5 million, is estimated at 12 megawatts, sufficient for Lesotho's own needs. Further expansions up to 17 megawatts would be possible. Preliminary findings indicate that the unit cost of electricity provided by the new plant would not be much higher than the ESCOM price. The government is seeking Canadian assistance for further studies, which are intended to include the identification of alternative sites than the Maltesunyane River, as a power plant there would destroy the tourism potential of Semonkong Falls.

Telecommunications

Lesotho's telephone system is operated by a department of the government. As all modes of communication in Lesotho, the telephone network is rather well developed in the lowlands along the north-south line more or less parallel to the west border with South Africa, although at both ends of this network there is considerable congestion. The existing network has a capacity of 2,500 lines. There are no east-west connections. Around 300 privately operated radio transmitters and receivers form part of the internal message systems operated by missions, traders, flying doctor services, and so forth. International connections are provided through South Africa.

In 1973 a Swedish expert, sponsored by SIDA, prepared a preliminary investment program for the period 1973/74-1980/81. The plan calls for upgrading the existing network and opening up rural areas in the foothills and mountains by constructing east-west links. Given the poor road connections in the mountain areas, adequate telecommunications are vital for good administration and represent an important social service. But because of the poverty of these areas, services will have to be largely subsidized. The plan also includes the building of a direct high-frequency radio link with Nairobi. This link, recommended earlier by International Telecommunications Union (ITU), would enable Lesotho to bypass South Africa for its international connections. Total costs of the plan are tentatively estimated at about R4 million. The governments of Sweden and Denmark will finance the first phase of the program.

H. Education

Formal education was introduced in Lesotho by missionary societies more than a century ago. The missions still run nearly all of the primary and secondary schools and all of the teacher training colleges (Table 5.5). Rivalries between the missions explain the large number of educational facilities, some with only a few pupils. There is no need for more institutions in the near future. The World Bank/Unesco reconnaissance mission in June 1973 estimated that there are twice as many primary schools as needed. Also, the background of the missionaries gave the educational system an academic bias; and, consequently, education was not really geared towards the development needs of the country. It should be noted, however, that the missions, often under difficult circumstances, have provided education to a large number of Basotho.

Table 5.5: NUMBER OF SCHOOLS, 1970

	Government controlled	Committee 1/ controlled	Mission controlled
Primary schools	1	15	1,071
Secondary schools	-	6	33
Teacher training	-	-	7
Technical and vocational training	1	-	10

1/ Committees with government representation.

Source: Ministry of Education, Annual Report 1971/72.

The missions' educational activities have given Lesotho a fairly high literacy rate. The 1966 population census defines literacy as the successful conclusion of two years of primary school and calculates the literacy rate at 47.5 percent for the whole population -- 32.9 for men, 50.1 for women. Literacy, however, is usually defined more rigorously; and, therefore, the literacy rate according to generally accepted norms is probably around 40 percent.

The large difference in literacy between men and women highlights also another characteristic of education in Lesotho. Many more girls than boys are enrolled in schools. The main reason for this is the use of young boys as herdboys.

Table 5.6: ENROLLMENT BY SEX

	Boys	Girls	Total
Primary schools (1972)	71,800	104,200	176,000
Secondary schools (1973)	5,976	6,599	12,575

Source: World Bank/Unesco reconnaissance mission.

Lesotho's schools suffer from a shortage of qualified teachers, poor facilities, inadequate equipment, a high proportion of children above school age, and an excessively high dropout rate. At the primary level only 12 percent of those who enter complete Grade 7, and at the secondary level 15 percent of those who enter complete the full five-year course. More than half of the secondary students stop after the third year, which gives them Junior Certificate level. The requirement to pay school fees and to purchase textbooks accounts for some of the attrition, but in large part it is due to poor teaching and inadequate facilities. Seventy percent of those completing

Grade 7 pass the examination, and 90 percent of those completing secondary school pass the Cambridge Overseas School Certificate examination. Thirty percent of the students completing primary school continue into secondary school. In terms of investment and expenditure, the high dropout rate is wasteful. There is also a large number of repeaters, estimated at about 20 percent of the pupils in primary schools. In 1971 the government introduced automatic promotion, but this system has met with resistance and does not seem to be enforced.

At primary level there are 4,000 teachers, 1,300 of whom are uncertified by the government's standards. At the secondary level there are 550 teachers, 145 of whom are uncertified and 105 are expatriates. It is the government's aim to replace all uncertified and expatriate teachers by 1980. Teachers' salaries were low compared to remunerations in other sectors of the monetary economy. Consequently, there was a high turnover rate, exceeding 30 percent per annum. The recent (60 percent) increase in qualified secondary teachers' salaries is expected to reduce the high rate of attrition. The planned salary increase in 1974 for qualified primary teachers should also stabliize that group.

Over the last five years, the government's recurrent expenditure has average R2.3 million a year, or 19 percent of total recurrent expenditure. Government capital expenditure was R0.2 million a year on the average, or 7 percent of the total (Tables 4.3 and 4.5). The missions' own expenditures on recurrent costs are assumed to be 10 percent of total operating costs of education, and in 1970 the missions' capital expenditures were almost as high as government capital expenditure. Although most of the schools are mission operated, government is aiding the missions with grants. Until recently grants were distributed in proportion to each mission's educational commitment, as calculated more than twenty years ago. In 1970 a new system was introduced whereby grants from the government were based on average attendance figures. The government has assumed an increasing share of the financial burden by paying these grants-in-aid. Aid to education also comes from other outside sources; they include teachers sponsored by the Peace Corps and under the United Kingdom assistance program; consultants under UNDP grants; a Rockefeller Foundation grant (US$250,000) to assist the School of Education at the University of Botswana, Lesotho, and Swaziland; and a school food program under the World Food Program.

The average teacher/student ratio in primary schools is 1:45, which is very high but much better than during the 1960s when it was 1:54. The average, however, hides far worse situations in some schools. It is the government's policy to lessen the number of primary schools and turn them into larger, more efficient units. The various religious missions, however, have been less than forthcoming in helping to achieve this.

Secondary education has a total enrollment of almost 13,000 pupils, which is 8 percent of the relevant 13 to 18 year age group. With 52.5 percent girls and 47.5 percent boys, the division of enrollment according to sex is far more equal than in primary schools. There are about 550 teachers, more than 25 percent of whom are without certificates; 20 percent are expatriate teachers. Secondary education still has the traditional academic bias, although greater attention is now being given to mathematics and science.

A mathematics-science center was opened in Maseru at the end of 1971; and a crash course has been started at the University of Botswana, Lesotho, and Swaziland to train science and mathematics teachers. Development of new curricula is well under way; and the government is planning to make a core curriculum of six courses consisting of Sesotho, English, mathematics, integrated science, development studies, and integrated skills compulsory for all secondary schools. The teacher/student ratio is reasonable (1:22 in 1972). The dropout rate after junior grade is very high (almost 60 percent). Some 1,300 students received their Junior Certificates, and almost 400 students received their Cambridge Overseas School Certificates in 1972.

To accomplish its goal of replacing all uncertified and expatriate teachers by 1980, the government needs 2,870 newly trained teachers -- 2,000 for primary schools and 870 for secondary schools. At present there are seven teacher training colleges, all operated by missions and aided by grants from the government. Enrollment in these colleges is around 350, and the annual output is at present 180 primary school teachers and 60 secondary school teachers. The colleges are small and inefficient, and output has to be increased greatly if the government's goal is to be met. The government plans to amalgamate all teacher training in a National Teacher Training College (NTTC). Denmark, the United Kingdom, and UNDP have agreed to finance this project, which will largely be implemented by Unesco. NTTC will offer a three-year post-Junior Certificate course and a two-year post-Cambridge Certificate course, as well as in-service training for uncertified teachers and curriculum development facilities. The secondary teacher training program of the University of Botswana, Lesotho, and Swaziland will also be expanded.

The only institution in Lesotho providing formal training in agriculture is the Lesotho Agricultural College. It offers a two-year post-secondary course and has an output of twenty technicians a year. The Swaziland Agricultural College, which forms part of UBLS, gives three-year diploma courses for higher education in agriculture. To satisfay the demand for middle-level technicians in agriculture, the capacity of the Lesotho Agricultural College should at least be doubled. The British government is likely to finance this.

Rural education, including all post-school training provided to adults, farmers, youth groups, and housewives, is at present poorly organized and fragmented. There are some farming training centers operated by the Ministry of Agriculture. A youth service training center operates under the Cabinet. Education through health and nutrition clinics is provided by the Ministry of Health; and there is a scattering of community development activity, also under the Cabinet. The government feels the economic and political necessity to organize adult education, especially in the rural areas, and to provide primary school leavers with skills which will contribute to rural employment. The government is considering the establishment of a rural development council, which would include the Ministries of Education, Health, Agriculture, Interior, and Planning. Its mandate would be to plan, organize, and administer an integrated rural education development scheme, which would include training in agriculture, health, crafts, nutrition, and home science, togather with assistnace in marketing, credit, community development, sanitation, and construction. The scheme would operate from existing primary schools, providing access to the entire population.

Vocational and commercial training is particularly weak in Lesotho. The Lerotholi Technical Institute (LTI) in Maseru offers three-year technical training courses in carpentry and mechanical trades. In 1971 the entrance level to LTI was raised from primary school to Junior Certificate (three years of secondary school) in order to improve the standards of the graduates. Present enrollment is about 120 students, and the annual output is 30. Most of the graduates are absorbed by the government. With a continuing development of the private sector, the demand for skilled craftsmen will no doubt increase. LTI in its present form is inadequate in terms of staff, buildings, and equipment and is not likely to produce the number and quality of craftsmen required. Also, it does not provide for the training of middle-level technicians. Improvement and expansion of LTI, in particular the addition of middle-level training, are urgently needed. Commercial training is presently being introduced at secondary schools, and the government plans to establish the Lesotho Institute of Business and Administration to meet the specialized needs in both the private and public sectors (see below).

The government is considering the establishment of an Inter-College Common Services Pool, which would incorporate all national post-secondary educational institutions. The rationale behind this is that instructor services and facilities could be shared among several institutions so that staffing costs and other overheads would be reduced and so that the quality of education in all units improved.

With the creation of the Rural Development Council and the Common Services Pool, the country's organization of educational services would be considerably streamlined. It would also be easier to handle policymaking and planning in education. Furthermore, the government is gaining more and more control over primary and secondary education by providing most of the finance needed for the schools. The government does not intend to take over actual administration and operation of the mission schools, but it wants to establish control over the curricula and teaching standards. Adequate teaching standards and the introduction of new curricula would be made a prerequisite for financial support to schools.

Following the visit of the World Bank-Unesco reconnaissance mission in June 1973, the government put together an education project for foreign financing that combines several of the elements discussed above and that would cater to Lesotho's most immediate, obvious manpower needs. The project includes: (a) the diversification of six secondary schools to provide prevocational, agricultural, handicrafts, and domestic science training; (b) the expansion of LTI to provide the full range of artisan and technician training; (c) the establishment of the Lesotho Institute for Business and Administration (LIBA); (d) the establishment of a national extension college to organize and administer an adult education program through formal and nonformal means; and (e) technical assistance for staff development and project implementation. The total project cost is estimated at R5.5 million (US$8.1 million). IDA would contribute with a credit of US$4 million towards the cost of the project. Various bilateral donors would provide another US$4 million, and the remainder of the cost would be borne by the government.

The main facilities of the University of Botswana, Lesotho, and Swaziland (formerly the Roman Catholic Pope Pius XII University College) are at Roma, 21 miles from Maseru. In 1971 UBLS commenced a process of devolution, and now the university has extended its physical presence to all three countries. The university offers four-year degree courses in arts and sciences and a three-year diploma course in agriculture (i.e., the Swaziland Agricultural College); there is also a school of education and a statistics department. Enrollment at the university's Roma campus is 465, of which about 150 are Basotho. The university is attempting to increase its development role and to adjust its education more to the needs of the three countries.

I. Banking

Before the Lesotho Bank started operations in October 1972, the banking sector in Lesotho was dominated by two foreign commercial banking groups -- the Standard Bank Limited and Barclays Bank International Ltd. Available banking statistics reveal that deposits are much larger than loans and advances, owing to the lack of what the commercial bankers consider to be bankable investment opportunities in Lesotho. The banks invest most of their surplus funds abroad. Most of the business advances in Lesotho have been to foreign industries and traders. So far, the commercial banks have hardly extended any credit to Basotho businesses. Lack of adequate collateral would have been the main obstacle. The lack of credit facilities for local entrepreneurs prompted the government to establish the Lesotho Bank, which started operations in October 1972 (see page 61). Until recently there was no banking legislation in Lesotho; but in January 1974 a financial institutions bill was passed, which provides, among other things, for the establishment of minimum capital, reserve and liquidity requirements, a comprehensive system of statistical reporting, and for the possibility to place government paper with the local banks.

Table 5.7: CONSOLIDATED COMMERCIAL BANKING STATISTICS, 1970-1973
(In million rand)

	Dec. 1969	Dec. 1970	Dec. 1971	Dec. 1972	June 1973
Cash on hand	0.5	0.6	0.7	0.8	-
Loans and advances	2.0	2.7	4.4	5.0	5.3
of which: Government	0.1	0.1	0.1	0.2	0.4
Private sector	1.9	2.6	4.3	4.8	4.9
Deposits	9.6	10.1	11.9	12.5	14.2
of which Government	-	2.3	3.1	2.6	3.2
Private sector	-	7.8	8.8	9.9	11.0
Other assets (mostly balances with head offices)	7.1	6.8	6.8	7.6	8.9 1/

1/ Includes cash on hand.

Source: Data provided by the Lesotho authorities.

Interest rates in Lesotho are generally in line with those in South Africa. With the exception of the government, which pays a concessionary 6 percent interest on its overdrafts, interest rates charged to borrowers vary from 8 to 12 percent, depending on the degree of security. Savings accounts with the commercial banks yield 3.5 percent interest, and time deposits from 4.5 to 7 percent.

Other financial institutions operating in Lesotho include branches of several South African building societies, such as those for agriculture (the Agricultural Development Fund -- ADF, Co-op Lesotho, and the Lesotho Credit Union Scheme for Agriculture -- LECUSA, as well as various small credit unions) (see page 45) and the Post Office Savings Bank (POSB), which in October 1972 was amalgamated with the Lesotho Bank. All insurance business is handled by South African insurance companies; but, as in the case with commercial credit, Basotho businessmen have hardly any possibility to get insurance. In order to fill this gap, the government is considering establishing a national insurance scheme.

The South African building societies accept savings depostis in Lesotho but have so far not invested there (see page 10). The ADF, Co-op Lesotho, LECUSA, and the various smaller credit unions were set up, mainly by foreign private sponsors, to provide possibilities for obtaining credit by farmers and small local businessmen. Because of management problems these institutions have generally not been very successful. In order to provide better credit facilities for local businessmen and farmers, the government passed legislation in March 1971 to set up the Lesotho Bank, which has been in operation since October 1972. A manager for the bank was provided by UNDP.

The fully government-owned Lesotho Bank was set up to mobilize savings and to fill the gaps in the domestic credit structure. It took over the assets and liabilities of the Post Office Savings Bank (POSB). POSB had an accumulated reserve of R88,000 at the end of 1972, which became part of the capital of the Lesotho Bank. Furthermore, the government contributed R530,000 in cash and ceded two loans -- R150,000 to LNDC and R400,000 to the Lesotho Electricity Corporation -- as additional paid-up capital.

The POSB has operated since April 1966. At the time of the takeover by the Lesotho Bank, its liabilities consisted mainly of deposits of small savers (R1.1 million) and the account of the Teachers' Provident Fund (R336,200). Since 1969 POSB has invested all of its funds within Lesotho. Investments included loans to the government, LNDC, the Lesotho Transport Fund, Maseru Water Supply, and the Lesotho Sports Council. Until the takeover, savings deposits with POSB remained at a level of about R1 million. Since then, however, deposits increased to R2.4 million by June 1973, mainly as a result of a relatively high interest rate on savings deposit (5 percent, as compared to 3.5 percent given by commercial banks) and as a result of an active campaign among civil servants to keep their savings accounts with the Lesotho Bank.

Although the Lesotho Bank has been successful in attracting local savings, it has not yet addressed itself to the task of providing credit facilities for farmers and small local businessmen. Instead, it has started acting as a normal commercial bank. The bulk of the Lesotho Bank's resources has so far been either loaned to public agencies, used to acquire property in Maseru, or deposited temporarily with the other commercial banks. The reason for not having lent in those sectors for which it was established are mainly severe staffing problems, which were exacerbated in July 1973 when the managing director of the Lesotho Bank was also put in charge of LNDC (see page 50). The government, however, remains anxious to let the Lesotho Bank evolve into a viable institution for development finance. If a revitalized LNDC succeeds in attracting new industrial and tourism enterprises, especially from outside South Africa, it would need long-term loan capital which could be channeled through the Lesotho Bank. As to credit to farmers and local businessmen, it would seem a logical step to establish an agricultural credit division which would consolidate the functions of the present various small agricultural credit institutions, and to attach the credit division of the Basotho Enterprises Development Corporation, if and when it is established, to the Lesotho Bank. Before the Lesotho Bank can assume its expanded role, however, serious efforts will have to be made to recruit suitable staff.

VI. OUTLOOK FOR DEVELOPMENT

At the beginning of the Second Five-Year Development Plan (April 1975), Lesotho will in many respects be much better prepared to embark on an ambitious development program than at the inception of the First Plan. In 1971 the First Plan could not be much more than merely indicative. Because of the lack of sector knowledge, it did not yet have a concrete, practical content; and, in any case, institutions inside and outside government needed to be built up and strengthened as vehicles for the implementation of the development programs. With the help of preinvestment studies and sector surveys undertaken in the recent past or planned to start soon and with experience gained with large-scale agricultural projects started since 1970, the government should be able to put together a sizable and realistic plan. As in the First Plan, the emphasis should be on the productive sectors -- particularly agriculture, industry, and tourism -- and on education to overcome the severe scarcity of educated and skilled manpower. Financial resources are not likely to be an important constraint. The bottleneck is likely to be the implementation capacity of the government. In the past increasing this capacity has been slow and difficult because of the government's policy to contain recurrent expenditures. With a much more buoyant revenue position than in the past (see pages 29-32), the government should use part of its financial resources to allow a controlled increase of recurrent expenditure directed at broadening the country's absorptive capacity.

Qualified and experienced local staff is scarce, and Lesotho is very dependent on foreign expertise. It is the government's intention to replace the numerous expatriate staff with nationals as soon as possible, but it does not want to do so until adequately trained local staff is available. The government, therefore, attaches high priority to further evolution of the regional university (UBLS), to make it more development oriented, and to emphasize fellowship programs for external training. Most fellowships offered in the past by donors had been tied to specific fields and projects and could by taken up only if a qualified candidate were available and could be spared from his job. This was frequently not the case, and many fellowships were not used. On the other hand, in other fields qualified Basotho were frequently available; but no fellowship was available. UNDP has recently made a provision for unallocated fellowships to help out, but the demands on the provision are far greater than financial resources available. Bilateral donors could greatly assist Lesotho in overcoming its trained manpower shortage by granting more untied fellowships than before.

In spite of all efforts, it will take considerable time before Basotho nationals will be available for all key positions in government administration and development planning and implementation. In the meantime, with a development program increasing in size, the government will be critically dependent on foreign technical assistance. The United Kingdom and UNDP have the largest technical assistance programs in Lesotho at present, but their financial and manpower resources are limited. Other donors, therefore, should be prepared to provide as much technical assistance as possible with the financial assistance they provide for projects. Ideally, such assistance should not be confined to the preparation and execution of the project itself;

it should be broader in scope, aimed at improving the capacity to plan and implement programs in sectors and ministries.

A. Financial Resources

As seen in Table 6.1, the mission estimated the financial resources available for the government investment program under the Second Plan 1975/76-1979/80 at about R85 million for the five-year period. The figures on foreign assistance are, of course, highly tentative. They are not so much based on actual commitments for the plan period as on extrapolations of present aid levels and indications of various agencies as to the level of aid that they would be willing to provide. The amount available could be higher if Lesotho concludes an association with the European Economic Community or if financial assistance from the oil-producing countries would be forthcoming. In contrast with the First Plan, the government of Lesotho is likely to be able to contribute substantially to the financing of its capital program, not only through budget surpluses but also through increased local borrowing if the necessary steps are taken to mobilize the financial resources that now flow abroad. With the estimated financial resources available, it would be possible to aim at a government capital investment program of some R17 million a year during the 1975/76-1979/80 period, which, in real terms, would be about twice the size of the program under the First Plan. Whether this level can, in fact, be achieved depends critically on the steps the government will take to increase its absorptive capacity (see pages 33-36).

Table 6.1: ESTIMATED FINANCIAL RESOURCES FOR GOVERNMENT INVESTMENT, 1975/76-1979/80
(In million rand)

Budget surpluses	20.0
U.K. capital grants	22.5
IDA credits	10.0
USAID grants and credits	5.0
Canada	7.5
Other donors	15.0
Local borrowing	5.0
Total	85.0

Source: Mission estimates.

In the past most of the capital assistance to Lesotho has been in the form of grants, and hence the public debt is very low. Since the government is able to draw on the foreign exchange earnings of the whole Southern African Customs Union to service its external debt, its creditworthiness depends on its budgetary position. Servicing of existing public debt amounted to R314,000 in the 1973/74 period, which represents a very low 1.5 percent of current revenue. Also in future Lesotho is likely to recieve most of its capital assistance in the form of grants of soft IDA-type credits. If the capital financing as stated in Table 6.1 materializes and assuming that two-thirds of the unspecified capital aid will be in the form of grants and the rest in the form of soft credits as well as that local borrowing will be at conventional terms, the servicing of public debt may increase to R890,000 by the 1979/80 period, still representing a comfortably low 2.2 percent of expected government revenue.

Table 6.2: PUBLIC DEBT AS OF MID-1973
(In million rand)

Foreign loans	8.43
of which U.K. Treasury loans	1.40
U.K. Bank loans	0.53
IDA credits	6.50
Domestic loans	0.69
Total	9.12

Source: Ministry of Finance.

Table 6.3: ESTIMATED SERVICE PAYMENTS ON PUBLIC DEBT, 1972/73-1979/80

	Current revenue	Service Payments: Existing debt		Service Payments: Existing and new debt	
	(Million rand)	(Million rand)	(Percent revenue)	(Million rand)	(Percent revenue)
1972/73	12.0	0.29	2.4	0.29	2.4
1973/74	20.6	0.31	1.5	0.31	1.5
1974/75	24.0	0.32	1.3	0.33	1.4
1975/76	25.0	0.33	1.3	0.36	1.4
1976/77	31.9	0.35	1.1	0.45	1.4
1977/78	38.1	0.31	0.8	0.56	1.5
1978/79	39.8	0.31	0.8	0.72	1.8
1979/80	40.9	0.30	0.7	0.89	2.2

Source: Mission estimates.

B. Growth of the Economy

The First Plan had as a target to attain an average annual rate of growth of gross domestic product of not less than 5 percent. In this event this target turned out to be too ambitious for the period 1970/71-1974/75, mostly because of the long lead time needed to prepare agricultural projects, the long gestation period of such projects, and disappointments in attracting foreign industrial and mining enterprises. The mission has attempted to make a projection of the growth of GDP which may realistically be expected up to the end of the Second Plan period (Table 6.4). Such a projection is of necessity highly tentative, as much depends on the degree with which the government manages to accelerate agricultural development with which it has made a good beginning and, with respect to industries and tourism, on the government's promotional activities and the willingness of foreign enterpreneurs to invest in Lesotho.

Table 6.4: TENTATIVE PROJECTION OF GDP AND GNP GROWTH, 1970/71-1979/80 (Constant 1970/71 prices)

	1970/71 (Million rand)	Annual rate of increase (Percent)	1979/80 (Million rand)
Rural Sector	25.6	2.4	31.7
Agriculture	19.0	2.5	23.7
Ownership of dwellings	5.2	2.0	6.2
Other rural activities	1.4	2.5	1.8
Other Sectors	16.9	6.3	29.3
Productive sectors	2.3	19.0	10.7
Mining	0.7	35.0	6.0
Manufacturing	0.7	15.0	2.5
Construction, public utilities	0.9	10.0	2.2
Service sector	14.6	5 to 6	23.6
GDP at factor cost	42.5	5.0	66.0
Indirect taxes less subsidies	5.0		7.0
GDP at market prices	47.5	5.0	73.0

Sources: Mission estimates.

As to agriculture, the mission has assumed that agricultural projects lead to a doubling of production in the project area over a gestation period of, say, seven years, which amounts to an annual rate of increase of 10 percent. Agricultural projects presently in execution or being started extend over some 10 percent of the country's farmland. If the government manages to extend the coverage to some 50 percent by the 1979/80 period, the growth of total agricultural output may then accelerate to 5 percent a year. The average growth rate over the whole period would be some 2.5 percent. In mining the mission assumes the establishment of a medium-size diamond mine as well as rehabilitation and encouragement of small-scale diamond production by local diggers. The 15 percent growth rate in manufacturing is an extrapolation of what might have been the growth rate in the last three years. It implies a continued success in attracting small industries of the type and size already established in Lesotho. If, however, the government manages to attract one or two large-scale enterprises, the growth rate of manufacturing production might well be twice as large or more, reflecting the still very low base in the 1970/71 period. The services sector could grow at a rate of

5 to 6 percent a year, mainly as a result of tourism development and of an expansion of government administration and services.

The projections of growth rates in the various sectors add up to a growth rate of GDP of 5 percent a year between the 1970/71 and 1979/80 period. This may not seem a very high rate of growth, but it should be borne in mind that it represents an average for the period. If agricultural development gradually covers a larger proportion of the country, the GDP growth rate may accelerate from virtually zero in the beginning of the period to almost 8 percent a year by the 1979/80 period.

The effect of the projected growth of the economy on wage employment in the modern sectors is not likely to be very substantial in absolute terms. Although wage employment within Lesotho might increase by some 7 percent a year between 1973 and 1980, this will absorb not more than about 17 percent of the expected increase in the total labor force, assuming that the latter grows as fast as the de jure population.

Table 6.5: ESTIMATED GROWTH IN WAGE EMPLOYMENT, 1973-1980

	1973 (Persons)	1980 (Persons)	Annual rate of increase (Percent)
Sectors			
Manufacturing	2,000	4,000	12
Mining	-	500	-
Construction, public utilities	1,000	2,000	10
Tourism	600	1.500	15
Government services	7,500	11,000	6
Other services	10,000	14,000	5
Total wage employment	21.100	33,500	7
Total labor force	450,000	524,000	2.2
Percent in wage employment in Lesotho	4.8	6.4	

Source: Mission estimates.

Even if the government succeeds in attracting a few large industries, the outlook would not alter substantially. In the foreseeable future Lesotho is likely to remain overwhelmingly dependent on South Africa's labor market. Nevertheless, about half of Lesotho's labor force, men and women, is at present at home, engaged mainly in small-scale agriculture and some informal enterprises (home industries and trading). While not neglecting to create as much wage employment as possible, an important element of the government's development effort should, in the mission's opinion, be directed at this segment of the labor force. For lack of development, the number of people available for work in the agricultural sector has declined substantially over the last six years (see page 18). If the government succeeds in keeping stable the labor force presently working on the land by making agriculture more attractive, the number of people leaving for employment in South Africa need not increase by more than 4 percent a year, as compared to 6 to 7 percent a year over the last decade or so.

Table 6.6: LESOTHO'S LABOR FORCE, 1973-1980
(Persons)

	1973	1980
Total labor force	450,000	524,000
Employed in the traditional sector	229,000	229,000
Wage employment in Lesotho	21,000	33,500
in South Africa	200,000	261,500

Source: Mission estimates.

The mission believes that the government has found the right answer with rural development projects of the type of the Leribe, Khomokhoana, Senqu, and Thaba Bosiu projects, all of which are aimed at improving the productivity of the small family farmholding. Initial indications are that these projects are successful. The scope of these projects could be widened by including the livestock industry. The advantages of the integrated rural development projects are that they are relatively simple, easily replicable, and capable of reaching a large proportion of the rural population at a relatively low cost, which is precisely what Lesotho needs. Even if the employment effect may initially not be very large, rural development should in the mission's opinion receive very high priority because (a) it is essential for erosion control; (b) it will, in any case, improve family incomes and provide better nutrition standards; and (c) it would secure a better basis to fall back on, should something go wrong with employment opportunities abroad.

The employment projections in Table 6.6 indicate that in the foreseeable future a substantial part of Lesotho's labor force will have to continue to find jobs abroad. In the above projections the mission has assumed that the South African labor market can absorb an additional 60,000 migrant workers over the next seven years or so. The mission, however, was not in a position to ascertain whether this is a realistic possibility. In the past Basotho labor was absorbed at an even faster pace, but increasing mechanization in the South African mines may slow down the rate of growth in employment opportunities for mine workers. The projections demonstrate clearly how vulnerable the stability of Lesotho economy and society is to conditions in South Africa over which Lesotho's government has no control.

This was brought home sharply in the first few months of 1974 when, because of as yet unexplained tribal clashes in South Africa, more than 14,000 migrant workers returned to Lesotho. A number of them have gone back to South Africa since then, but nevertheless the government is suddenly faced with the problem of providing relief for thousands of unemployed. This recent massive return of migrant workers may or may not be a temporary phenomenon. Even if it is temporary, it may occur again. The government, therefore, has started preparing a number of labor-intensive projects -- such as soil conservation, road construction and maintenance, and afforestation, which could be carried out quickly if and when the need arises and for which the government is seeking technical and financial assistance from multilateral and bilateral agencies.

Even if employment opportunities for Basotho in South Africa do not increase as fast as projected, or not at all, a substantial number of Basotho will continue to work in South Africa. Under these circumstances the government might wish to consider giving more assistance to migrant workers. A realistic emigration policy would imply not only market research into the most remunerative possibilities for migrant workers in South Africa or elsewhere but also provision of technical training. Ideally, the government's education policies should, therefore, aim not only at overcoming domestic manpower constraints but also at improving the earning capacity of Lesotho's large migrant labor force. At present Lesotho exports mainly unskilled labor. However, the demand in South Africa for skilled and trained workers is large, and their wages are two to three times as high as those of unskilled workers. If such policy is acceptable to the government, the issue arises as to how to recover the cost of services provided to migrant workers. Because of the training and other services provided, the government would have a justifiable right to tax its residents working abroad. Perhaps the easiest form of taxation would be a form of labor tax to be paid directly to the government by employers abroad.

APPENDIX:

STATISTICAL TABLES

Table 1.1: POPULATION, 1891-1966

(In thousand persons)

Census	African Population			Other	Total
	Resident	Absent	Total		
1891	218.5	..	..	0.6	..
1904	347.9	..	..	0.9	..
1911	402.9	24.6	427.5	1.6	429.1
1921	497.0	47.1	544.1	1.8	545.9
1936	560.5	101.3	661.8	1.8	663.6
1946	561.9	..	..	2.0	..
1956	639.5	154.8	794.3	2.2	796.5
1966	850.5	117.3 a/	967.3 a/	2.4	969.7 a/

a/ Under-enumerated; actual figures are thought to be 40,000-50,000 higher.

Source: Bureau of Statistics, Census Reports.

Table 1.2: RESIDENT AFRICAN POPULATION BY SEX AND AGE GROUP, 1966

(In thousand persons)

Age Group	Males	Females	Total
00 - 14	185	185	370
15 - 29	71.	117	188
30 - 44	43	75	118
45 - 59	41	56	97
60 - 74	22	36	58
75 and over	5	14	19
Total	367	483	850

Source: Bureau of Statistics, Census Report 1966.

Table 1.3: BASOTHO WORKING IN SOUTH AFRICAN GOLD MINES AND COLLIERIES: NUMBER, DEFERRED PAY, AND REMITTANCES, SELECTED YEARS, 1950-1973

Year	Basotho Workers ('000)	Deferred Pay (million rand)	Remittances (million rand)
1950	34	0.4	0.3
1955	44	0.5	0.7
1960	51	0.7	0.8
1965	68	1.1	1.1
1970	89	2.5	2.2
1971	87	3.0	2.0
1972	99	3.4	2.4
1973	111	..	..

Source: Bureau of Statistics.

Table 2.1: ESTIMATES OF GDP AT FACTOR COST, 1966/67-1970/71 a/

(In million rand and at current prices)

	1966/67	1967/68	1968/69	1969/70	1970/71
Rural sector	24.7	24.1	26.4	26.3	25.4
Agriculture	18.8	18.1	20.4	20.1	19.0
(of which subsistence)	(13.2)	(12.7)	(14.2)	(14.1)	(13.3)
Ownership of dwellings	5.8	5.9	6.0	6.2	6.4
Industry	2.4	3.0	2.8	3.2	3.4
Mining, quarrying	0.7	1.0	0.6	0.9	0.7
Manufacturing, crafts	0.8	1.0	1.0	1.0	1.3
Construction	0.8	0.9	1.0	1.1	1.1
Public utilities	0.1	0.1	0.2	0.2	0.3
Services	12.1	14.1	14.5	14.8	13.7
Commerce, catering	5.1	5.8	5.8	5.6	5.1
Transport, communications	0.4	0.5	0.5	0.6	0.7
Banking, insurance, etc.	0.5	0.6	0.5	0.8	0.5
General government	3.3	4.0	4.3	4.4	4.3
Education	1.6	1.9	2.0	2.0	1.9
Health	0.5	0.6	0.6	0.7	0.6
Other services	0.7	0.8	0.7	0.7	0.6
Total GDP at factor cost	39.2	41.3	43.7	44.4	42.5

a/ Figures may not add to total because of rounding.

Source: Bureau of Statistics.

Table 2.2: ESTIMATES OF DOMESTIC EXPENDITURE, 1966/67-1970/71

(In million rand and at current prices)

	1966/67	1967/68	1968/69	1969/70	1970/71
Consumption	55.3	58.4	62.3	62.9	65.1
Private	49.9	51.3	55.6	56.0	57.7
Government	5.4	7.1	6.6	6.9	7.4
Gross capital formation	4.4	5.3	5.2	5.2	5.5
Buildings and construction	2.3	2.7	2.6	2.3	2.2
Vehicles)		1.2	1.6	1.6	2.0
Plant, machinery, equipment)	1.7	0.5	0.4	0.7	0.6
Other	0.2	0.2	0.1	0.2	0.2
Change in stocks	0.3	0.6	0.5	0.5	0.5
Domestic expenditure	59.7	63.7	67.5	68.1	70.6

Source: Bureau of Statistics.

Balance of Payments

Table 3.1: RECORDED TRADE FIGURES, 1967-1972

(In thousand rand)

	1967	1968	1969	1970	1971	1972
Exports						
Cattle	1,202	1,101	579	684	606	686
Sheep and other animals	40	141	68	137	94	258
Wheat	33	179	426	927	140	140
Peas and beans	462	161	219	127	187	503
Other foodstuffs	35	24	19	11	12	47
Wool	1,480a/	1,513	1,426	912	774	2,040
Mohair	545a/	593	740	572	504	1,122
Hides and skins	98	79	46	24	22	48
Diamonds	1,017	376	1,174	652	241	196
Other	23	21	194	191	434	1,053b/
Total	4,935	4,188	4,891	4,237	3,014	6,093
Imports						
Foodstuffs and livestock	4,584	4,624	5,500	5,982	5,640	10,071
Beverages and tobacco	863	837	1,243	1,186	1,256	1,616
Crude materials	441	388	337	314	579	529
Mineral fuels and lubricants	1,605	1,153	1,399	1,476	1,723	2,440
Animal and vegetable oils	154	126	89	198	277	381
Chemicals	1,740	1,702	1,541	1,273	1,845	2,172
Manufactured goods	10,698	11,331	9,880	8,799	11,901	20,721
Machinery and transport equipment	2,495	2,557	2,839	3,058	4,114	5,042
Other	1,220	1,220	1,079	590	662	-
Total	23,800	23,938	23,907	22,876	27,997	42,972

a/ Estimates.

b/ For breakdown, see table 3.2.

Source: Annual statistical bulletins.

Table 3.2: CLASSIFICATION OF "OTHER EXPORTS," 1972

(In thousand rand)

Type of Goods	Value
Tapestry	150
Doors and frames	320
Cosmetics	64
Pottery	42
Lamp shades	32
Plasma	320
Paint	10
Candles	75
Semiprecious stones	20
Other	20
Total "other exports"	1,053

Source: Bureau of Statistics.

Table 3.3: EXPORTS OF SELECTED COMMODITIES, 1965-1972

	1965	1966	1967	1968	1969	1970	1971	1972
Cattle (thousand head)	11.9	13.0	13.4	18.4	15.3	11.4	8.7	8.9
Sheep and goats (thousand head)	10.7	9.1	5.4	16.5	25.9	16.1	10.9	31.8
Wheat (thousand bags of 200 pounds)	122.9	33.0	5.7	22.1	109.5	150.1	23.4	18.4
Wool (million pounds)	9.5	9.4	9.0	10.2	10.2	10.4	7.0	7.9
Mohair (million pounds)	2.2	2.4	2.2	2.5	2.5	2.1	1.9	1.8
Diamonds (thousand carats)	7.4	12.5	21.7	11.9	29.8	16.5	6.8	9.0

Source: Bureau of Statistics.

Table 4.1: EXTERNAL PUBLIC DEBT a/ OUTSTANDING AS OF DECEMBER 31, 1972

(Debt repayable in foreign currency, thousand US$)

Type of debt	Disbursed only	Including undisbursed
Total external public debt b/	8,338	8,338
Privately held debt by banks and financial institutions	1,083	1,083
South Africa	520	520
United Kingdom	563	563
Loans from international organizations	4,451	4,451
IDA	4,451	4,451
Loans from governments	2,804	2,804
United Kingdom b/	2,804	2,804

a/ Debt with a maturity of over one year.

b/ Net of accumulated sinking funds: United Kingdom, $714,000.

Source: World Bank, Economic and Social Data Division, Economic Analysis and Projections Department, August 6, 1973.

Table 4.2: OUTSTANDING EXTERNAL DEBT AND ESTIMATED SERVICE PAYMENTS, BY YEAR, 1968-1992
(In thousands of US$)

Year	Outstanding Debt 1/		Commit-ments	Disburse-ments	Service Payments			Cancel-lations, Adjust-ments
	Disbursed only	Including undisbursed			Principal	Interest	Total	
1968	4,376	6,448	1,053	2,122	82	175	257	-25
1969	6,391	7,394	413	861	115	155	270	-19
1970	7,116	7,673	429	144	314	218	532	184
1971	7,130	7,972	108	458	127	145	273	228
1972	7,713	8,181	-	468	149	227	376	306
1973	8,338	8,338	-	-	155	191	346	-150
1974	8,033	8,033	-	-	194	210	404	-45
1975	7,795	7,795	-	-	186	202	388	-46
1976	7,564	7,564	-	-	238	191	428	-27
1977	7,300	7,300	-	-	252	179	430	-9
1978	7,039	7,039	-	-	211	148	359	-10
1979	6,819	6,819	-	-	217	121	338	-10
1980	6,591	6,591	-	-	223	115	339	-11
1981	6,357	6,357	-	-	225	109	334	-5
1982	6,126	6,126	-	-	232	102	334	-
1983	5,894	5,894	-	-	240	88	328	-
1984	5,654	5,654	-	-	249	73	322	-
1985	5,405	5,405	-	-	258	64	322	-
1986	5,147	5,147	-	-	345	55	400	-
1987	4,753	4,753	-	-	273	42	316	-
1988	4,480	4,480	-	-	259	38	297	-
1989	4,221	4,221	-	-	252	35	287	-
1990	3,970	3,970	-	-	251	32	283	-
1991	3,719	3,719	-	-	249	30	279	-
1992	3,469	3,469	-	-	241	27	268	-

1/ At beginning period.

Source: Economic and Social Data Division, Economic Analysis and Projections Department, August 6, 1973.

Table 5.1: CENTRAL GOVERNMENT BUDGETARY POSITION, 1966/67-1973/74

(In million rand)

	Average 66/67-68/69	69/70	70/71	71/72	Preliminary 72/73	Mission Est. 73/74
Current revenue	5.2	9.0	9.1	11.1	12.0	20.6
Current expenditure	11.3	11.4	11.9	12.4	13.8	16.5
Current deficit/surplus	-6.1	-2.4	-2.8	-1.3	-1.8	+4.1
Capital expenditure	3.0	1.8	2.1	3.8	3.1	5.0
Financing deficit/surplus	-9.1	-4.2	-4.9	-5.1	-4.9	-0.9
Financed by:						
Grants						
U.K. grants-in-aid	5.2	1.6	2.0	0.9	0.6	-
U.K. capital grants a/	2.4	1.0	2.0	3.2	2.0	3.7
Other	0.4	0.5	0.5	0.4	0.1	1.0
Foreign loans						
IDA	0.9	0.1	-	-	-	0.5
UNDP	-	-	-	-	-	0.3
Domestic borrowing	0.1	0.1	0.6	0.3	0.4	0.2
Change in cash position	-0.1	-0.9	+0.2	-0.3	-1.8	+4.8

a/ Including those from private sources.

Source: Treasury annual reports and information provided by the Ministry of Finance.

Table 5.2: CENTRAL GOVERNMENT CURRENT REVENUE, 1966/67-1973/74
(In millions of rand)

	Average 66/67-68/69	69/70	70/71	71/72	Preliminary 72/73	Mission Est. 73/74
Direct taxes	1.3	1.7	1.9	2.4	2.6	2.8
of which						
Basic tax	0.9	0.9	1.0	1.0	1.0	1.1
Graded tax	-- a/	0.1	0.2	0.0	0.0	0.0
Personal income tax	0.4	0.6	0.3	0.7	1.0	1.1
Company tax			0.2	0.3	0.3	0.3
Development levy	-	0.1	0.2	0.2	0.3	0.3
Licenses and duties	0.4	0.5	0.4	0.5	0.4	0.5
Earnings of ministries and departments	1.0	1.0	1.1	1.4	1.4	1.6
Other local revenue	0.7	0.7	0.9	1.0	0.8	1.1
Total local revenue	3.4	4.0	4.4	5.2	5.3	6.0
Customs and excise	1.8	5.0	4.7	5.9	6.7	14.6
Total	5.2	9.0	9.1	11.1	12.0	20.6

a/ Indicates less than R50,000.

Source: Treasury annual reports and information provided by the Ministry of Finance.

Table 5.3: CENTRAL GOVERNMENT RECURRENT EXPENDITURE, 1966/67-1973/74
(In millions of rand)

	Average 66/67-68/69	69/70	70/71	71/72	Preliminary 72/73	Mission Est. 73/74
Economic services	2.5	2.3	2.6	3.0	3.3	4.1
Agriculture	0.9	1.0	1.1	1.2	1.3	
Public works	1.0	0.8	1.0	1.1	1.4	
Post and telecommunications	0.5	0.4	0.4	0.5	0.5	
Other a/	0.1	0.1	0.1	0.1	0.1	
Social services	3.2	3.2	3.0	3.3	4.0	5.0
Education	2.1	2.2	2.1	2.2	2.8	
Health	1.1	1.0	0.9	1.0	1.2	
Internal Security	1.3	1.6	1.9	1.9	1.8	2.3
Police	1.0	1.3	1.6	1.5	1.5	
Prisons	0.3	0.3	0.4	0.4	0.3	
General administration	3.1	3.0	3.1	3.4	3.9	4.6
Financial obligations	1.2	1.2	1.3	0.9	0.8	0.9
Public debt service	0.2	0.2	0.2	0.2	0.3	0.3
Other b/	1.0	1.0	1.1	0.7	0.5	0.6
Total	11.3	11.4	11.9	12.4	13.8	16.5

a/ Commerce, industry, mining, tourism and Maseru Town.
b/ Mostly pension obligations to former British officials.

Source: Treasury annual reports and information provided by the Ministry of Finance.

Table 5.4: CENTRAL GOVERNMENT CAPITAL EXPENDITURE, 1966/67-1972/73

(In million rand)

	Average 66/67-68/69	69/70	70/71	71/72	Preliminary 72/73
Productive activities	0.61	0.66	0.69	1.19	0.45
Agriculture	0.57	0.60	0.64	1.02	0.43
Mining, commerce, industry	0.04	0.06	0.05	0.17	0.02
Infrastructure	1.80	0.73	0.77	0.99	1.51
Roads	1.33	0.37	0.35	0.53	0.79
Public utilities	) 0.47	0.25	0.25	0.33	0.44
Other	)	0.11	0.17	0.13	0.27
Social services	0.24	0.21	0.27	0.40	0.31
Education	0.12	0.13	0.20	0.25	0.24
Health	0.12	0.08	0.07	0.15	0.07
General government services	0.35	0.17	0.41	1.25	0.87
Civil servants housing	-	-	-	0.30	0.17
Other	0.35	0.17	0.41	0.95	0.70
Total	3.00	1.77	2.14	3.83	3.14

Source: Treasury annual reports and information provided by the Ministry of Finance.

Table 5.5: FIVE-YEAR DEVELOPMENT PLAN, CAPITAL EXPENDITURE BY SECTOR, 1970/71-1974/75
(In thousand rand)

	1970/71	1971/72	1972/73	1973/74	1974/75
Productive activities	602	2,359	1,932	2,053	1,849
Agriculture and cooperatives	502	1,322	1,521	1,634	1,561
Industry (LNDC factory area development)	100	550	150	200	200
Commerce	-	142	76	23	23
Tourism	-	54	65	65	65
Mining	-	291	120	131	-
Economic infrastructure	875	1,442	2,016	2,096	1,786
Roads	518	842	1,483	1,982	1,677
Civil Aviation	17	155	22	22	22
Electricity	70	70	70	70	70
Post and telecommunications	270	275	86	22	17
Plant pool	-	100	355	-	-
Social infrastructure	643	1,410	2,959	2,283	1,285
Education and training	231	776	1,581	1,211	265
Health	160	137	214	162	157
Water supply, sewerage, sanitation	249	471	1,075	811	744
Sports	-	-	70	80	100
Minor urban services	3	26	19	19	19
General government services	519	919	555	715	504
Police, prisons	146	181	191	159	172
Office buildings	190	359	201	465	252
Public service housing	105	308	54	54	55
Other	78	71	109	37	25
Total	2,639	6,130	7,462	7,147	5,424

Source: Lesotho First Five-Year Development Plan, 1970/71-1974/75.

Table 6.1: CONSOLIDATED COMMERCIAL BANKING STATISTICS, 1969-1973

(In thousand rand)

	Dec. 1969	Dec. 1970	Dec. 1971	Dec. 1972	June 1973
Demand deposits	2,987	2,344	2,515	3,413	3,417
Government	673	299	367	289	569
Personal	1,420	646	1,196	2,003	2,612
Business	894	1,399	952	1,121	236
Savings deposits	3,379	3,602	3,958	4,393	4,784
Government	30	28	16	14	8
Personal	2,784	3,563	3,799	4,014	4,552
Business	565	11	143	365	224
Time deposits	3,149	4,223	5,396	4,709	5,961
Government	1,098	2,004	2,710	2,352	2,615
Personal	1,703	2,097	2,371	2,133	3,082
Business	348	122	315	224	264
Total deposits	9,515	10,169	11,869	12,515	14,162
Total advances	1,951	2,693	4,427	5,015	5,254
Government	100	107	78	204	400
Personal	686	809	864	935	2,292
Business	1,165	1,777	3,485	3,876	2,562

Source: Data provided by the Lesotho authorities.

Table 6.2: LESOTHO NATIONAL DEVELOPMENT CORPORATION ASSETS AND LIABILITIES, 1969-1973[a/]

(In thousand rand)

	1969	1970	1971	1972	1973
Assets	81	755	1,405	2,581	2,915
Fixed assets	6	14	132	515	914
Investments and loans	71	471	842	345	502
Shares in companies	71	72	117	309	373
Loans	-	399	725	36	129
Current assets	4	270	431	1,721	1,499
Fixed deposits	-	75	75	1,005	1,130
Call deposits and cash	4	127	262	575	204
Other	-	68	94	141	165
Liabilities	81	755	1,405	2,581	2,915
Accumulated funds	80	356	772	1,610	2,004
UK expenditure grants	44	79	79	79	79
UK capital grants	71	72	105	105	105
Reserve funds	-	-	60	417	681
Net profit	-30	205	528	1,009	1,139
Long-term loans	-	389	628	949	846
Current liabilities	1	10	5	22	65

a/ Each year as of March 31.

Source: LNDC annual reports.

Table 6.3: LESOTHO NATIONAL DEVELOPMENT CORPORATION PROFIT AND LOSS ACCOUNTS, 1969-1973[a]

(In thousand rand)

	1969	1970	1971	1972	1973
Income	3	287	494	1,022	605
Commercial and service agreements	2	270	412	404	417
Exploration leases	-	-	1	511	-
Interest on loans	1	10	60	19	15
Interest on deposits	-	3	16	73	101
Rentals	-	4	4	15	70
Sale of assets	-	-	1	-	2
Expenses	26	47	111	184	212
Interest on loans	-	9	43	58	53
Administration	26	38	48	79	118
Other	-	-	18	47	41
Profit in year	-23	240	383	838	393
Accumulated profit	-35[b]	205	588	1,366	1,402
less:					
Appropriation to reserve funds	-	-	60	357	263
Accumulated net profit	-35	205	528	1,009	1,139

a/ For years ended March 31.

b/ Including a loss of R12,000 in previous years.

Source: LNDC annual reports.

Table 6.4: LESOTHO BANK[a/], ASSETS AND LIABILITIES, 1966-1973

(In thousand rand)

	1966	1967	1968	1969	1970	1971	1972	1973
Assets	888	1,044	1,076	1,045	1,038	1,120	2,218	3,073
Investments	837	1,015	1,015	1,015	995	1,081	2,089	2,764
Cash and bank balances	10	15	47	11	4	17	86	64
Other	41	14	14	19	39	22	43	245
Liabilities	888	1,044	1,076	1,045	1,038	1,120	2,218	3,073
Paid-up capital	-	-	-	-	-	-	550	550
Reserve fund	-	20	24	41	61	79	88	88
Deposits	880	1,014	1,041	992	963	1,026	1,640	2,430
Other	8	10	11	12	14	15	10	5
Details of investments								
Nat. Industrial Credit Corp. (S.A.)	330	140	180	-	-	-	-	
Lesotho Government	-	175	175	320	320	320	320	
LNDC	-	-	-	233	600	600	650	
Lesotho Sports Council	-	-	-	-	-	26	102	
Maseru Water Supply	-	-	-	-	-	-	90	
Lesotho Transport Fund	-	-	-	-	-	-	170	
Lesotho Electricity Corporation	-	-	-	-	-	-	400	
Bank deposits	507	700	660	462	75	135	357	

a/ The Lesotho Bank commenced operations in September 1972 and took over the assets and liabilities of the Post Office Savings Bank. Figures before 1972 refer to the Post Office Savings Bank.

Source: Annual reports of the Post Office Savings Bank and Lesotho Bank.

Table 6.5: LESOTHO BANK[a/] REVENUE AND EXPENDITURE, 1966-1972

(In thousand rand)

	1966	1967	1968	1969	1970	1971	1972
Revenue	19	69	57	70	72	72	80
Interest on investment	19	68	57	70	72	72	80
Agency fees	-	1	-	-	-	-	-
Expenditures	20	48	53	53	52	54	71
Interest credited to depositors	12	38	41	39	38	38	54
Administration expenses	8	10	12	14	14	16	17
(Loss)/Profit	(1)	21	4	17	20	18	9
Transfer to Reserve Fund	-	20	4	17	20	18	9
Reserve Fund at end year	-	20	24	41	61	79	88

a/ See footnote table 8.3.

Source: Annual reports of the Post Office Savings Bank and Lesotho Bank.

Table 7.1: SIZE OF HOLDINGS OF FARM HOUSEHOLDS, 1950, 1960, 1970

	1950		1960		1970	
Size of Holdings (acres)	No. of Holdings	% of Holdings	No. of Holdings	% of Holdings	No. of Holdings	% of Holdings
0.0 - 3.9	53,520	36	68,746	44	92,481	50
4.0 - 7.9	59,620	40	55,747	36	63,131	34
8.0 - 14.9	29,920	20	24,879	16	24,861	13
15.0 - and over	6,740	4	5,915	4	4,603	3
Total	149,800	100	155,287	100	185,076	100

Source: Census of Agriculture 1950, 1960, and 1970.

Table 7.2: NUMBERS OF LIVESTOCK 1950, 1960, 1970

(In thousands)

	1950	1960	1970
Cattle	401	546	551
Sheep	1,564	1,466	1,655
Goats	637	672	974
Horses	103	135	110
Donkeys	59	97	90
Mules	3	7	4
Pigs	36	61	66
Chickens	..	771	841

Source: Bureau of Statistics.

Table 7.3: CROP STATISTICS, 1950-1972

	1950	1960	1970	1971	1972
Acres planted ('000)					
Maize	443	404	319	370	296
Sorghum	139	169	204	210	173
Wheat	122	167	263	272	235
Peas	21	43	30	35	30
Beans	6	14	40	44	37
Barley and oats	8	11	3	..	..
Crop production ('000 m.t.)					
Maize	214	121	67	121	64
Sorghum	49	54	57	78	59
Wheat	50	58	58	76	57
Peas	8	12	5	5	4
Beans	1	1	4	4	3
Yields (200 lb. /acre)					
Maize	5.3	3.7	2.3	3.6	2.4
Sorghum	4.0	3.8	3.1	4.1	3.8
Wheat	4.5	3.8	2.4	3.1	2.7
Peas	4.5	3.3	1.8	1.6	1.4
Beans	1.5	1.6	1.0	1.1	1.0

Source: Agricultural Censuses 1950, 1960 and 1970 and data provided by the Lesotho authorities.

Table 8.1: ELECTRICITY STATISTICS, 1970-1973[a/]

	1970	1971	1972	1973
Number of consumers	839	898	1,159	1,308
Units purchased and generated ('000)	7,806	9,606	13,452	17,510
Units sold ('000)	7,144	8,891	12,525	..
Annual maximum demand (kwh)	2,190	2,687	3,389	4,552
Annual loan factor	40.7	40.8	45.3	..

a/ Years ended March 31.

Source: Lesotho Electricity Corporation.

Table 9.1: URBAN RETAIL PRICE INDEX, JANUARY 1973-APRIL 1973

(October 1972 = 100)

Commodity Group	Low Income Households[a/]		All Households	
	Jan. 73	Apr. 73	Jan. 73	Apr. 73
All items	100.9	105.8	101.0	105.2
Food, drinks	100.9	107.5	100.6	106.8
Housing	100.0	107.2	100.0	104.2
Fuel, light, heat	102.1	102.9	101.7	102.6
Furniture, household goods	101.4	107.6	101.7	108.4
Clothing	100.6	104.8	100.4	103.8
Footwear	100.8	97.4	101.3	98.0
Medical and personal care	100.5	104.3	100.8	106.9
Transport	100.5	100.7	102.0	102.1
Other goods and services	101.0	105.6	101.4	105.9

a/ Annual income below R500 a year.

Source: Bureau of Statistics.

Table 10.1: MOTOR VEHICLE REGISTRATION, 1972

	Number		
	New registration	Re-registration	Total
Private cars	458	1,498	1,956
Combies	67	169	236
Vans	319	884	1,203
Landrovers	123	468	591
Trucks	100	447	547
Buses	30	105	135
Tractors	150	668	818
Motorcycles	34	111	145
Trailers	73	268	341
Total	1,354	4,618	5,972

Source: Annual Statistical Bulletin, 1972.